CONTENT MARKETING COUP

DESKTOP BATTLE BOOK

DANE BROOKES

First Edition: April 2016

Published by Giant Leap Media

ISBN-13: 978-0993369728

ISBN-10: 0993369723

For my beloved grandparents:

Alfred and Irene, Josephine and John.

Thank you for your love, lessons and immeasurable legacy.

CONTENTS

INTRODUCTION

"First gain the victory and then make the best
use of it you can."

Horatio Nelson

I was inspired to write my first business book, *Content Marketing Revolution*, after experiencing first-hand many of the successes and failures marketers and business owners make with marketing.

As the founder of international marketing agency, *Group Dane*, I work with many different types of companies, in a range of sectors. If there is one thing I've noticed about virtually everyone I've ever worked with, from FTSE 100 marketing directors to one-man-bands, it is that time is never in abundant supply. This book aims to provide swift guidance on the most important elements of content marketing planning, execution and monitoring. It is designed to give you a quick steer on the task you're working on at the moment and provide a sense check for your decisions. Keep it on your desk and use it as you need to. I have left space for you to make notes where necessary.

For more information and analysis on any of the points I cover in this *Desktop Battle Book*, refer to my book *Content Marketing Revolution*, or search for me online.

WHAT IS CONTENT MARKETING?

First things first, let's make sure we agree on the definition of content marketing. The following definition comes from *Content Marketing Revolution*:

> Content marketing involves creating, sourcing and targeting specific audiences with valuable and engaging content. The aim is to establish long-term relationships with new and existing customers that ultimately generate profitable actions. It can be used at every stage of the buyer's journey and crosses all channels, platforms and formats, including online, print, in-person, in-place, mobile and social.

While traditional marketing aims to sell with overt sales and persuasive messaging, content marketing helps consumers to feel more empowered in their decision making. By providing content that is valuable on an informative, useful or entertaining level, businesses can form relationships with customers that lead to more sales and increased buyer satisfaction.

WHY "COUP"?

It's no secret that we are in the midst of the greatest marketing revolution since the advent of the internet. Look around and you'll see evidence of it everywhere in the form of high-value content being published by brands of all sizes, within all sectors.

This marketing revolution is being driven by an unprecedented cultural shift in consumer behaviour. More than ever before, customers want to make empowered decisions based on useful information, valuable engagements and brand affinity.

Right now, you have an opportunity to seize control of your market by building lasting, profitable relationships with more customers through highly-relevant content.

HOW TO USE THIS BOOK

Throughout the book, each section includes prompts for important actions you'll need to perform along your journey, together with snippets of insight that will help to point you in the right direction. I would recommend reading the book in its entirety, then keeping it on your desk to refer back to throughout the course of your daily, weekly or monthly activities. With this in mind, each section has been carefully designed to give you all of the important information as concisely and directly as possible.

For your convenience, every website, service and tool I recommend or reference is indexed alphabetically at the end of the book.

TIME FOR ACTION

Over the following pages, I will highlight the specific actions you'll need to take to drive the most effective, efficient and measurable outcomes.

By following the guidance in this book, you'll be equipped to stage your very own market coup, build lasting audience relationships and win over the hearts and minds of your target customers.

Be the revolution!

Dane Brookes

London, 2016

1

RESEARCH

"Knowledge has to be improved, challenged
and increased constantly, or it vanishes."

Peter Drucker

Research is a crucial part of every content marketing strategy. But,
there's no point wasting valuable time and effort gathering
intelligence you're never going to use, so it is important to focus
your attention only in the areas that matter.

Before you do anything, you need to get a clear picture of the
current situation in your market. You're going to need to find out
what content is already out there, identify the hot topics of
discussion, work out where people are looking for content,

recognise which individuals and brands have the most influential voices, and pinpoint your main content competitors.

Armed with this information, you'll be best placed to judge what kind of content the market will respond to.

In order to gather this information, you'll need to get a little closer to your target audience by immersing yourself in the customer's world.

TAP INTO THE CONTENT COMMUNITY

You may not realise it, but your target audience is already part of a "content community". This community is made up of everyone with an interest in your area of business, including prospective and existing customers; experts and authorities in the field; bloggers and commentators; and, of course, competitors.

A good understanding of your content community will give you an insight into the likes and dislikes of your audience. By watching, reading and listening to what people are saying, you can establish how they feel about important topics and what their values and priorities are.

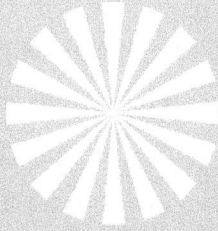

RESEARCH ACTION #1

Make a list of what your target customers are saying about your product or service area, including the problems it solves and the sentiments expressed. Concentrate on the following factors:

1. What are the key points being made?
2. What are the questions being asked?
3. Who is answering the questions and offering advice (e.g. fellow customers, competitors, etc)?
4. Is there any content being linked and recommended in response to problems and issues raised in public forums?

SOCIAL RESEARCH

One of the best ways to get a reliable insight into your community is by simply searching social networking sites, such as Facebook, Twitter, Google Plus and LinkedIn. Look for information that will help you to discover the key questions being raised by the community, who is currently answering these questions and specifically what types of content is being shared.

MONITOR CONVERSATIONS IN REAL-TIME

Supplement manual keyword searches by monitoring relevant conversations in real-time by using social media listening tools like Hootsuite and Social Mention.

AUDIT COMMUNITY CONTENT

Before you start thinking about your own content, it's important to get a solid picture of what is already out there. Here, you need to be looking specifically for content related to your product or service type, taking into account the predetermining reasons people are motivated to buy.

COUP INSIGHT

Broadly, there are three types of community content to look for:

1. Content focussed on the problem or reason people might be interested in your product or service.
2. Content that helps people with the process of choosing the right solution.
3. Content related to the post-purchase stage.

CONTENT CONSUMPTION

Use the content that's already out there as a litmus test for your own ideas. What existing content (your own and third-party) is the most popular and which pieces seem to be sinking into the abyss?

Take a look at how widely the content is shared across social media, using tools like Socialcrawlytics and Shared Count, which track how widely specific URLs have been shared, liked and tweeted.

You can also get a reasonably accurate picture of how much traffic third-party website content is getting using SEMrush, which uncovers a whole host of data about your competitors' digital marketing strategies.

Use all of this information to forecast how your audience will respond to certain topics and content types before investing any time or money into developing them.

CONTENT SEARCH

Not all of the content your customers are looking for is already out there. You can find out what information (or entertainment) they are looking for by investigating the popularity of relevant keywords used in search engines. The frequency in which certain terms and phrases appear will help you to work out what topics your customers are most interested in.

Using Google Trends, you can drill-down on search patterns by country, region or city, while also revealing the most popular related words and phrases. By plotting a search term's popularity over time, you can identify which topics are growing in popularity and which are gradually being searched for less.

Figure 1: Google Trends

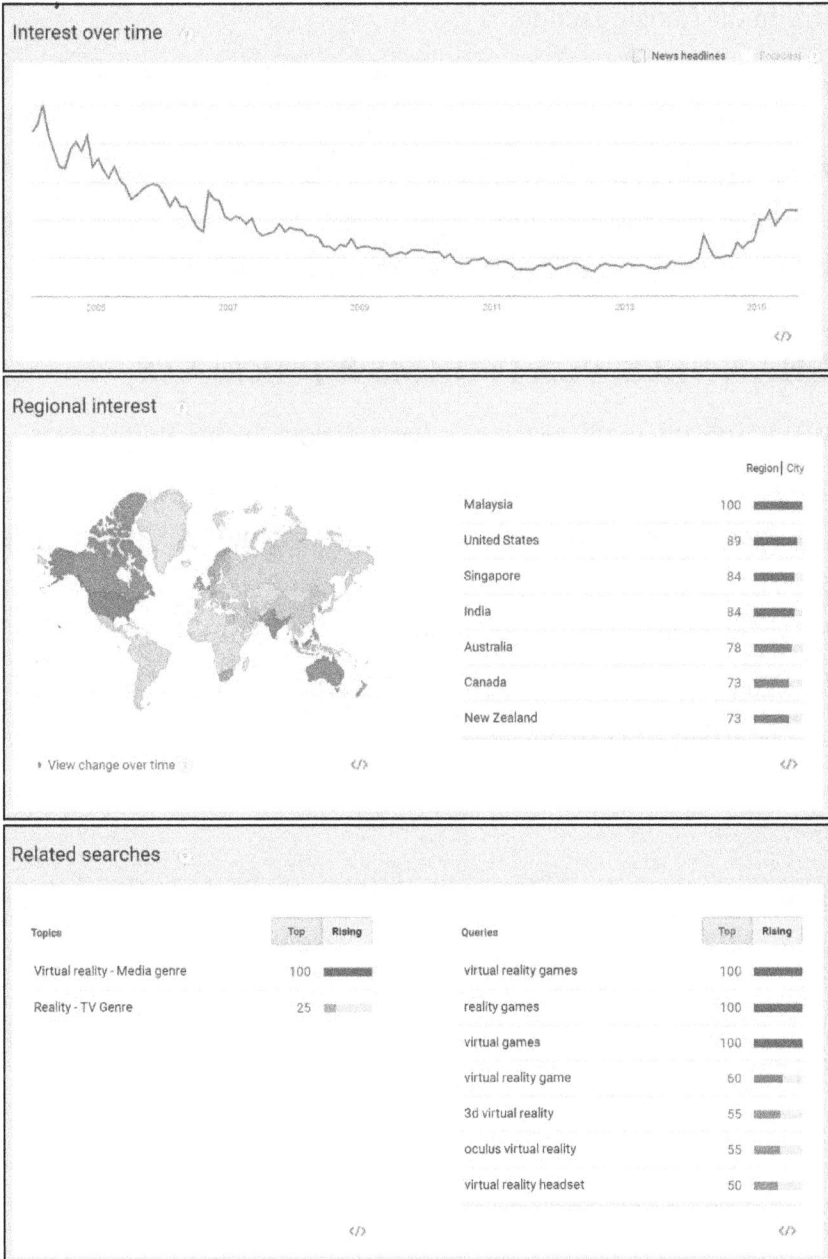

Interest over time

Regional interest

	Region	City
Malaysia	100	
United States	89	
Singapore	84	
India	84	
Australia	78	
Canada	73	
New Zealand	73	

▸ View change over time

Related searches

Topics	Top	Rising	Queries	Top	Rising
Virtual reality - Media genre	100		virtual reality games	100	
Reality - TV Genre	25		reality games	100	
			virtual games	100	
			virtual reality game	60	
			3d virtual reality	55	
			oculus virtual reality	55	
			virtual reality headset	50	

Source: Google Trends © www.google.com/trends

Figure 1 shows results returned for a search on 'virtual reality', within the Google Trends.

You can gather yet more insight by using the 'forecast' option in the viewing panel. This reveals predictions for future search volumes, which can help you to generate ideas around topics that are likely to become more popular over time, thus pre-empting your audience's content needs in advance of your competitors!

CHANNELS, PLATFORMS & FORMATS

What websites and social networks is your community using to access specific content types (e.g. videos, blogs, PDF guides, etc.)?

Again, by using social reach monitoring tools like Socialcrawlytics and Shared Count, you can find out which content types and channels are most popular.

You will quickly start to see which types of content are popular and how they are being used.

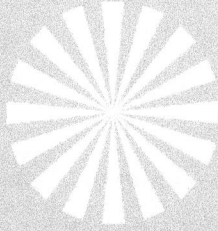

RESEARCH ACTION #2

As you trawl your content community, record the details of each piece of content you assess. Create three separate lists:

1. Channel
2. Platform
3. Format

IDENTIFY INFLUENCERS

Engaging with the most dominant and persuasive voices in the market is one of the top three priorities of most content marketers. We call these voices, which can be individuals, groups or brands, 'influencers'.

The two main benefits of engaging with influencers are:

1. increasing your brand profile (by association); and
2. giving your content the biggest potential for amplification (i.e. sharing and reaching large volumes of target customers) across the internet.

Influencers, as the name suggests, have the power to evoke certain thoughts, values and actions among the target group, so it is important that you know who they are and, ideally, have them on your side.

As you research your community more, you will start to see which individuals and brands have the most valued, authoritative voices in the field. You can also use systems like Klout to identify and rank influencers according to specific topics, which you can then compare against your own influence ranking.

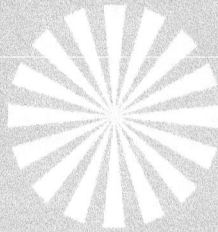

RESEARCH ACTION #3

Based on all of the insights you have gathered so far, try to identify the main influencer(s) in your community.

1. Who have the most dominant, authoritative voices (this could be individuals or organisations)?
2. Are there any topics that these key influencers are focussing on? List them.

CONTENT COMPETITORS

Your competitors in content marketing may not be the same as your competitors in business.

Identify who is making the most noise and gaining the most engagements with customers on websites, blogs and social media? These are the voices you will be competing with when you start to publish content, so gather as much information about them as possible.

Using Google Alerts, you can arrange to receive notifications when new relevant content is published anywhere on the internet. If necessary, you can even keep tabs on specific authors and domain names.

If you already have some of your own content out there, it is worth comparing how it performs against other leading voices in your community, using tools like QuickSprout.

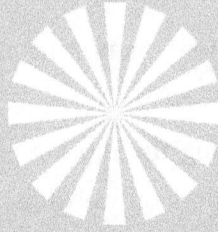

RESEARCH ACTION #4

As you give more attention to what's happening in your content community, you'll start to see the same content producers popping up over and over again. There may be one clear leader, or there may be a few. Gather as much information as possible about their content activities so you can answer the following questions:

1. How frequently are they publishing?
2. What are their specific focuses and niche topics?
3. How much content are they producing weekly/monthly?
4. How well is their content received by the community (look at comments, shares, etc)?
5. Are there any obvious gaps in their provision? If so what?
6. How much of their content relates to current market issues and trends?

MISSION SUMMARY

High-quality research is one of the most important weapons you will ever have in your content marketing armoury. Not only will it help you to better target your efforts and therefore save valuable resources, it will also highlight those big opportunities where you can make an impact.

The revolution you are planning in your marketplace will be bolstered by the intelligence you gather at the start and throughout the process. Don't be put off by what might seem like an arduous and complex task; focussing your research in the areas you have discussed will pay dividends later.

2

CONTENT INVENTORY

*"Every right implies a responsibility;
Every opportunity, an obligation,
Every possession, a duty."*

John D Rockefeller

Many individuals and organisations pump out lots of different types of content over a period of years, without ever realising the volume. Over time, this content can be forgotten about and left drifting until a potential customer stumbles across it. It is important to recognise that poor-quality, inaccurately-messaged and out of date content can be just as damaging to your brand as good content can be beneficial.

In the case of good content, an inventory can alert you to the possibilities of reusing, repurposing or re-promoting it where relevant.

Your content inventory should include content that has been created for both internal and external audiences, old and new content and even content you might feel is irrelevant. It is important to record all formats, from leaflets and flyers, to blog posts and videos.

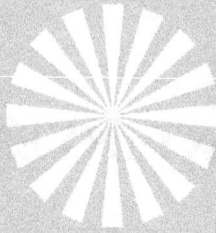

INVENTORY ACTION #1

Create an inventory document containing all of the fields mentioned above. Use spreadsheet software (such as Microsoft Excel), set up an online document (such as Google Docs), or download the free template on the *Content Marketing Coup* website.

There are a number of online tools that can help with your content inventory, such as Screaming Frog and Blaze, but, creating an inventory manually, using a Microsoft Excel spreadsheet or a Google Doc can be just as effective.

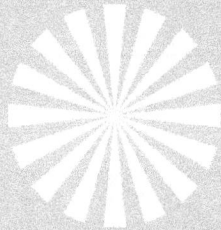

INVENTORY ACTION #2

Cataloguing every single piece of content you currently have, recording the following information for each:

- Content ID (give it a unique number for reference purposes).
- Name (the title of the content, e.g. 'Top Tips on SEO').
- Content type (e.g. blog post, web page, leaflet).
- Location (URL or physical location).
- Format (e.g. video, text, eBook, etc.).
- Publish status (is this currently available? YES/NO).
- Content owner (who in the business is responsible for this content?).

Figure 2: Example content audit and inventory worksheet

ID#	NAME	CONTENT TYPE	LOCATION	FORMAT	PUBLISHED	OWNER	REVIEW BY	ACTION
101	Top 10 tips on SEO	Blog post	www.example.com/...	Webpage/HTML	Y	A.E. SMITH	10.10.17	REVIEW
102	Content Marketing into	Video	www.example.com/...	FLV	Y	F. WILLIAMS	10.10.17	REVIEW
103	State of the Creation	Whitepaper	www.example.com/...	PDF	Y	I.M. SMITH	10.10.17	RETAIN
104	Intro to making money online	Podcast	www.example.com/...	MP3	N	J.M. SMITH	05.03.16	REVIEW
105	Myth killers: Who wants	Blog post	www.example.com/...	Webpage/HTML	Y	E. McMannus	05.03.17	RETAIN
106	Dave Cartwright interview	Podcast	www.example.com/...	MP3	Y	A.E. SMITH	10.10.17	REVIEW
107	Welcome to the content	SlideShare	www.example.com/...	PPT	Y	J. WANG	10.10.17	REVIEW
108	Grant Cardone interview	Podcast	www.example.com/...	MP3	Y	C.P. MORTIMER	10.10.17	RETAIN
109	How to figure out the	Video	www.example.com/...	MPEG 4	N	K. DOWN	05.03.16	REVIEW
110	Get up, stay up	Blog post	www.example.com/...	Webpage	Y	D. HOLT	05.03.17	RETAIN
111	The future of virtual	Whitepaper	www.example.com/...	PDF	Y	D. HOLT	10.10.17	REVIEW
112	Top 3 ways to improve	Flyer	www.example.com/...	Print leaflet	Y	K. DOWN	10.10.17	REVIEW
113	Content Marketing Rev	eBook	www.example.com/...	PDF	Y	I.M. SMITH	10.10.17	RETAIN
114	Life fixer: who wants	Email epsiode	www.example.com/...	Email	Y	J.M. CULL	05.03.16	REMOVE
115	How to make best use	Manual	www.example.com/...	PDF	Y	F. WILLIAMS	05.03.17	RETAIN
116	The only links you'll	Links page	www.example.com/...	Webpage/HTML	Y	J. TURPIN	10.10.17	REVIEW
117	Oculus Fox: The magazine	Magazine	www.example.com/...	Print mag	N	J. COOK	10.10.17	REVIEW
118	Oculus Fox: The magazine	Magazine	www.example.com/...	Print mag	N	A.E. SMITH	10.10.17	RETAIN
119	Oculus Fox: The magazine	Magazine	www.example.com/...	Print mag	Y	D. HOLT	05.03.16	REVIEW
120	Oculus Fox: The magazine	Magazine	www.example.com/...	Print mag	Y	K. DOWN	10.10.17	RETAIN
121	Train the trainer: a live	Webinar	www.example.com/...	Quicktime	Y	C.P. MORTIMER	10.10.17	REMOVE
122	The future of content	Infographic	www.example.com/...	PNG	N	E. McMannus	10.10.17	REVIEW
123	The history of content	Infographic	www.example.com/...	PNG	N	J. WANG	10.10.17	RETAIN
124	How to sell more of the	Infographic	www.example.com/...	PNG	Y	K. DOWN	10.10.17	REVIEW
125	Facebook: is it the best	Case study	www.example.com/...	Webpage/HTML	Y	J.M. CULL	05.03.16	RETAIN
126	Free stock photography	Stock photos	www.example.com/...	JPG	Y	I.M. SMITH	05.03.17	REMOVE

3

CONTENT AUDIT

"Be a yardstick of quality. Some people
aren't used to an environment where
excellence is expected."

Steve Jobs

Once you have created a complete inventory of the content you
own, it is important to thoroughly assess it.

A content audit will help you to determine just how useful (or
damaging) any of the content could be to your content strategy and
your business in general. This involves assessing and grading every
item according to its topical focus, quality, level of usage and how it
relates to your overall content marketing strategy.

AUDIT ACTION #1

Look at each piece of content and give it a score (use any grading system you like, e.g. 1-5 stars). Here are the main questions you need to ask yourself:

1. How well executed is the content (is it well written, appropriately professional to its context, etc.)?
2. Is the content in keeping with your brand and style guide?
3. How useful is the content in relation to its purpose?

USAGE AND ANALYTICS

Obviously, we only create content because we want it to be read, viewed or listened to. The top question on your mind should always be *whether* and *how* your content is being used by your target audience.

However, the insights you gather about usage can only be used as a measure of success if you look at them in relation to how the content was intended to be used and by how many people. In other words, success can only be determined by relating performance to target. For example, if you created the content for a small niche audience group, your analytics will probably reflect that – but low figures in this case could represent more success than a campaign that has huge viewing figures if the target was a lot bigger.

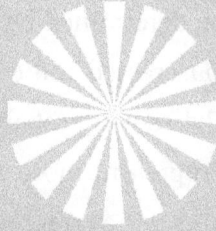

AUDIT ACTION #2

Look at each piece of content and try to determine what portion of your target audience it might appeal to. Now think about what channels this was published on and how much it was promoted in a targeted way.

There are three main factors to think about:

1. How many people was the content exposed to through promotion, the channel it was published on, etc? Use any information you can gather from social media analytics (e.g. how many news feeds did this show up in?), along with any other stats you have for things like number of impressions, views of promo pages, etc.
2. Of this pool of people exposed to your content, how many of them would you realistically expect to be interested in it? Consider the title, subject matter and presentation.
3. How many people actually read, viewed or watched the content?

BUYER PERSONAS

All of the content you publish should be created for specific customer segments or groups. If you aren't familiar with the concept of buyer personas, or you don't already have some to work with, return to this action after you have covered *Buyer Personas* in section 4, page 33.

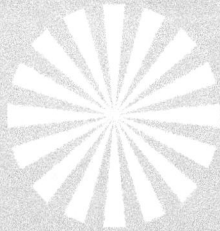

AUDIT ACTION #3

Map every piece of content in your inventory to one or more of your buyer personas. Think about how each piece specifically appeals to the buyers. Does it help, interest or entertain them?

This will help you to identify:

1. Content that doesn't appeal to any of your personas.
2. Audience groups that are under-served by your content.
3. General gaps in your content provision.

BUYER STAGE

If your content is truly relevant to your target audience and it helps to support your overall marketing strategy, it must fit into your ideal buyer's journey. Some pieces of content will support more than one buyer stage, some might even fit into every stage, but it should fit *somewhere*.

If you aren't familiar with the concept of the buyer's journey, or you haven't already planned out your buyer's journey, return to this action after you have covered the *Buyer's Journey* in section 5, page 61.

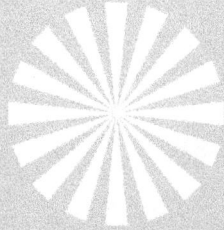

AUDIT ACTION #4

Go through every piece of content and map each piece to a specific stage in the buyer's journey.

This will help you to identify any stages of the buyer's journey that are underrepresented by your content. You may not need an even spread of content throughout each stage of the buyer's journey, but you may find that certain stages are less supported by your content than others.

CONTENT STATUS AND FATE

It's time to make some bold decisions; every piece of content in your inventory needs a designated fate!

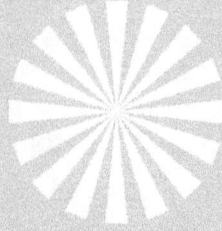

AUDIT ACTION #5

Look at each piece of content and decide what you're going to do with it, marking it accordingly in your existing inventory database:

1. **Remove:** If the content is redundant, out of date, or irrelevant, you need to cut your losses and get rid of it.

2. **Repair:** Maybe the content is still relevant or valuable in some way, but needs some work to improve it or make it more relevant to your overall marketing goals. Remember to make a note of specifically what needs fixing.

3. **Replace:** Is the content valuable in principle, but flawed in its execution? In this case, mark it for replacement and add a note about why it needs to be redone.

4. **Retain:** This content is perfectly fine; you will leave this as it is.

GAP ANALYSIS

Once you have completed the audit, you can start to look for content gaps. What else do your buyer personas need? Are you missing anything obvious? This information will help to guide content ideas later.

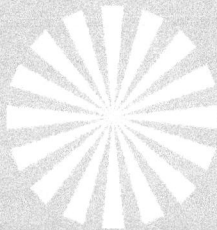

AUDIT ACTION #6

Based on what you discovered in Audit Actions #3 (buyer personas) and #4 (buyer's journey), identify the gaps in your existing content provision. This will be useful later when you're developing ideas for new content.

Create two lists:

1. Which of your personas are not served effectively by your content?
2. Which stages of the buyer's journey are under-supported by your existing content?

MISSION SUMMARY

With a fully catalogued and reviewed content portfolio, you will be better placed to make judgements about new content and keep on top of existing assets. In the process, you're also likely to stumble across off-radar content that can be re-used. Just as importantly, you will also be more responsible publishers, with a clear idea of what content is out there representing your brand.

Most people are generally nervous about getting rid of content because of the amount of work that went into creating it. But, you need to be bold and remove the dead wood that is weighing down your portfolio. Think about the potential customers who may only ever have one touch point with your brand. Are you confident that *this* piece of content represents you in the best light? If not, pull the plug and start over.

4

BUYER PERSONAS

*"Market to your best customers first,
your best prospects second and
the rest of the world last."*

John Romero

Buyer personas are essentially fictional characters that are created to represent main customer groups, which can be used to help inform sales and content strategies.

While personas don't tell you everything you could ever wish to know about your target audiences, in my experience they are the most useful way to understand and interpret customer behavioural patterns, motivations and goals.

Having a set of well-formed personas will help us to focus on exactly the types of people we are creating content for, why they want or need it, how they will access it and what actions it is likely to motivate.

How many buyer personas you need will depend on how many distinct audience segments you need to represent. You're not looking for different *types of people* that make up our customers; you're looking for broad groups of *customer motivations*.

The key information you should include in each buyer persona depends on the industry and product types, but they typically include things like:

- Gender and age range.
- Location.
- Educational and career level.
- Profession, specialism and industry.
- Wherewithal/budget/financial circumstances.
- Interests outside of the product remit.
- Shopping habits.

You can gather demographic data relatively easily from any customer or lead data you already have, by conducting online or offline customer surveys and looking at website visitor statistics (with tools such as Google Analytics) and social media insight data (Facebook, Twitter and LinkedIn all provide built-in analytics).

Though demographic data is useful, you need to dig a lot deeper if your personas are going to be of any real value. It is difficult, if not impossible, to accurately attribute demographic information, such as gender and age, to the factors that motivate customers without directly asking your audience through surveys or interviews. After all, your aim is not to create an interesting representation of your audience; you are looking to create a tool that highlights key customer needs. Your aim is to elicit the ultimate motivations that influence buying decisions for your main customer groups, e.g. how, when and why the buyer decides to choose you or a competitor.

According to Adele Revella, author of *The Buyer Persona Manifesto*, the questions you ask when developing your personas need to be framed around five key areas of insight. Adele created the *Five Rings of Buyer Insight* to help draw out the key factors that will define your personas:

1. PRIORITY INITIATIVES

What causes certain customers to invest in a solution like yours, and how are they different from customers who remain attached to the status quo?

In other words, what is really on the buyer's radar? To use an IT example, knowing how old his system is, you may think your buyer is obsessed with replacing it. Meanwhile, what actually keeps him up at night is fear that the entire department will move to India. Too often, you arrogantly presume that since what you do is important to you it must be just as important to the buyer. The truth is out there, find it.

But don't confuse this with 'pain points' and assume you can simply reverse-engineer based on the capabilities of your solution. You want to understand the personal or organisational circumstances that cause your customers to allocate their time, budget or political capital to resolve the 'pain'. What happens to make this investment a priority for this type of buyer?

2. SUCCESS FACTORS

What operational or personal results does your buyer persona expect from purchasing your solution?

Success Factors resemble benefits, but this insight is far more specific and it's written from the buyer's perspective. For example, where you might be pushing your solution's power to cut costs, this insight might focus on where the buyer sees opportunity to reduce business risks.

Done right, this insight yields a far more specific and compelling set of factors than anything you can reverse-engineer from the capabilities of your solution. Instead of ending up with a ten-word tagline or summary that sounds just like your competitors, you will be armed with a concise statement of your customers' key expectations.

3. PERCEIVED BARRIERS

What concerns cause your buyer to believe that your solution or company is not their best option?

Adele Revella calls this the "bad news insight" because it tells you exactly why this buyer will not buy from us. It could be internal resistance from another function or scars from prior experience. It could be a negative perception of your product or company, accurate or not.

You need to know where the barriers are and what's behind them. Who is blocking you further up the ladder? Where is that negative impression coming from, social media perhaps?

As a result, you may be surprised to find that your most valuable content focuses on overcoming these barriers and addressing objections that your competitors didn't know were there.

4. THE BUYER'S JOURNEY

This reveals the behind-the-scenes story at each phase of the evaluation.

Who is involved? How are solutions evaluated? How does the process unfold as the decision gets made? This insight tracks the stages that your customers go through as they evaluate options, eliminate contenders and settle on a final choice.

Behind-the-scenes, this can be a very messy process. Your key buyer persona may live in a complex ecosystem that includes all sorts of characters who have a hand in decision-making at various stages of the journey. Who helps your key persona and who gets in their way? You're often surprised to find that the people at the top of the totem pole have less clout than vendors assume.

With an accurate understanding of the journey, you can support your buyer with exactly what is needed at each stage. And you can confidently commit your resources where they will have maximum impact, be it social media, content marketing, sales engagement or something entirely creative.

5. DECISION CRITERIA

Which aspects of the competing offerings do your customers perceive as most critical and what do they expect from each one?

This final insight directly informs marketing messaging and content, clarifying the buyer's key questions and the answers they want to hear. But it's equally critical for sales enablement, as it identifies which customers care about specific features and why.

For example, if the buyer wants an 'easy-to-use' solution, you dig to find what they mean by that. Where do they want that ease? How do they go about evaluating which solution is easiest?

You usually focus on revealing the criteria behind three to five capabilities that matter most to the buyer in question. For example, specific product features, implementation issues or price versus value calculations.

Source: Adele Revella, The Buyer Persona Manifesto.

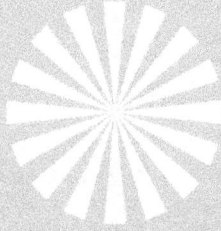

PERSONA ACTION #1

Use all of the data and insights you have collected about your customers so far to identify:

1. The priority problems that are big enough to push buyers to your product.
2. The level of investment your buyer places in your solution (e.g. how much time, effort and money are they willing to invest to solve the problem?)
3. The constraints the buyer faces that your solution helps them with (e.g. lack of time, lack of budget, etc).

PERSONA ACTION #2

Now identify the specific outcomes and results your customers expect from your product or solution. Remember, we're focussing only on *your* products or services here.

Write one or more short statements that broadly describe your customers' expectations. There may be one statement that fits all customers, or there may be several statements that reflect different types of customers.

PERSONA ACTION #3

What is the "bad news insight" for you? Identify the reasons you have found that are stopping prospective customers from buying, along with barriers that are blocking repeat sales from existing customers.

1. Make a list of all negative perceptions your target customers have about your products or services
2. Assign each negative perception to a root. Where did this come from? (For example, perhaps there is a negative perception about your products because of conversations on social media in your community.)

CONDUCTING INTERVIEWS

How do you go about gathering the kind of information you'll need to create a set of solid buyer personas? The only way is to get up close and personal with your audience. You need to conduct interviews with a representative cross-section of current and prospective customers.

FACE-TO-FACE

Interviewing is the only reliable method of gathering in-depth audience insight. Being in the room with the customers allows for flexibility and enables you to adapt your approach based on the individual needs of the participant.

All of the information that forms your buyer personas must come from research; nothing should be plucked from thin air. Given that your interview intelligence will form the basis of your personas, it is essential that you ask the right people the *right questions*.

WHO TO INTERVIEW

- **Customers:** It makes sense to start with existing customers; they are already buying your products and services. It is important to focus both on happy customers and dissatisfied customers. Unhappy customers don't buy again, so it is useful to find out exactly how their behaviour differs from happier ones. Do they have different needs or attitudes? Are they just not your target audience?

- **Prospects:** Naturally, you will also want to know as much as possible about the needs, motivations and behaviours of your prospective customers. By definition, you don't have a business relationship with these people yet, so you will need to work harder on tapping into these groups. Any information you hold on prospects will help you to identify and reach out to potential interviewees. It's a good idea to start with any lead generation data you have, customer service queries that didn't end in a close and any social media interactions we've had with non-customers.

If you don't have any leads in to prospective customers, you can use free monitoring services like Mention and Talkwalker Alerts to monitor what people are saying about products and services in your field. It will take some further digging to identify whether or not they are genuine prospects, but if they are suitable, it's worth considering inviting them to take part in your research.

Remember that the purpose of your contact with these people is to conduct research and not to make a sale. Explain this from the outset and only talk about your products or services if they ask.

COUP INSIGHT

You could make life easier and save time by interviewing staff and friends. But you aren't looking for an easy life; you're looking for reliable representative data. Avoid interviewing anyone who falls into the following groups, because their answers will be at best skewed and at worst useless:

- Staff at the company.
- Friends and family.
- People outside of the target group.
- Non-customers with a vested interest (including supporters, haters and product reviewers).

HOW MANY PEOPLE?

There is debate about how many interviews will provide a reliable insight. Some, like Adele Revella, suggest that just six to ten interviews will provide enough data to identify trends, while Kim Goodwin, author of *Designing for the Digital Age*, suggests you need at least twelve. Personally, I have never interviewed less than eight or more than twelve for any one exercise.

ALWAYS IN-PERSON

All of your interviews must be held in-person. If you can't see the interviewee, you will miss out on valuable unspoken insights, such as facial expressions and body language. Plus, in my experience, interviewees are more open and receptive to questioning when you have eye contact.

THE PERFECT SETTING

A relaxed and comfortable participant is a more open and honest participant. The setting of your interviews is almost as important as your questions. The top three considerations are privacy, neutrality and seating proximity:

1. **Privacy:** When most people think about a relaxed and informal setting, they think about a coffee shop or a quiet bar, perhaps with a piano man in the corner. Although this sounds mellow, it's not a good setting for an interview. You don't want any distractions, such as people walking past or noisy coffee machines, to interrupt your participant's line of thought. Always, always go for a private room.

2. **Neutrality:** You should never hold the interviews on your own premises. Psychologically, the participant feels like a guest and may be less comfortable passing negative comments.

3. **Seating proximity:** The seating arrangement is more important than most people think. The participant should always be seated nearest to the exit, with a clear route out of

the room. It sounds odd, but, psychologically, this will help to relax the participant, as they don't feel trapped and can quickly escape the situation!

THE RIGHT INTERVIEWERS

Interviewing is a skill. If budget allows, get professional help with interviews. Not only will expert interviewers already have the skills required to tease out useful responses, participants are often more likely to be honest with a third party.

COUP INSIGHT

Remember that the information you gather from interviews will form the foundations of your personas, so make sure the interviewers you choose are the right people for the job.

A skilled interviewer has the three Es in abundance: energy, empathy and examination skills. Choose your interviewers using the following as a 'job description':

1. **Energetic:** Maintaining energy during the interview is crucial if you are going to provoke detailed responses. Energy and enthusiasm are contagious, so a powered-

up interviewer will keep the interviewee's mind active and engaged. Thinking can be strenuous; just think of the fatigue you feel after an exam.

2. **Empathetic:** Although the interviewer should try to avoid leading the interviewee's responses, building an empathetic rapport will help to put the interviewee at ease. Simple gestures like nodding, smiling and pausing make a big difference. Remember, when people are comfortable, they are usually more open.

3. **Examining:** All good interviewers are naturally curious and comfortable with going off-piste to further probe ambiguous or interesting responses.

FRAMING QUESTIONS

You need to frame your questions carefully in order to get the most expansive and honest answers. Your questions should give your interviewees the freedom to express their thoughts rather than simple "yes" or "no" responses.

COUP INSIGHT

Broadly, there are three stages of prompts to use in interviews. Devise your question using variations of the following examples.

1. **Example early-stage prompts:**
   - Can you please tell me how you came to...?
   - What were the events that led up to...?
   - What happened after you...?

2. **Example mid-stage prompts:**
   - Was anyone else involved in your decision to...?
   - Can you help me to understand how you go about...?
   - What were the most important things you learnt about...?

3. **Example end-stage prompts:**
   - Can you tell me how your views have changed since...?
   - Is there anything you can add to help me better understand...?

THE DICTAPHONE IS MIGHTIER THAN THE PEN

Always record the interviews on a Dictaphone. You won't notice anything interesting about the participant's reactions if you are looking down at a pen and paper. After the interview, you can transcribe the audio recording verbatim and pick up on emotional indicators like tonality and hesitation. Do they really mean what they are saying?

Q&A TAG TEAM

Whenever I'm involved in interviews, I employ a system that my team call the 'Q&A Tag Team'. It allows all of the verbal and non-verbal responses to be captured without having to use a video camera (in my experience video cameras tend to throw interviewees' concentration and affect the quality of their responses).

For each interview, you'll need two interviewers working together and switching roles after each question.

This is how it works: Interviewer #1 should ask the first question, recording the response on a Dictaphone. While the participant is answering the question, Interviewer #2 should make notes about visible emotional reactions, such as facial expression and body language, anchoring these notes to certain points in the answer.

TRANSCRIPTION

Transcribing the Dictaphone recording isn't the most exciting task of the project, but it is worth putting in the time and effort to ensure you don't miss any key nuggets of insight. Along with the verbal responses, include information about intonation and use

Interviewer #2's notes to include details about facial expressions and body language. This will help you to understand the underlying emotions connected to the answers.

CREATING BUYER PERSONAS

Once you have completed the interviews, you'll have a pile of data that will need to be sorted and interpreted. This may feel like an overwhelming task at first, but following a systematic approach will help you to run through the data and pull out all of the key information.

AFFINITY DIAGRAMS

The first step in piecing all of this together is to create affinity diagrams with the interview responses. This method will help you to organise large amounts of data into natural groups.

PERSONA ACTION #4

Follow the steps below to organise all of the information you have gathered about your customers into an affinity diagram.

1. **Find key points:** Go through the notes for each interview one-by-one and write the main points on individual cards or Post-it notes. Take care to include the emotional states where necessary (including verbal, facial and body language signals). Each point should be at least a noun and verb, preferably a phrase. For example, one note might say "Product too expensive" or "Not sure if it's right for me".

   On each card or Post-it note, write initials or numbers that will help you to link the specific point to the interviewee it originates from.

2. **Group:** Put all of the Post-it notes onto a wall or table and group similar ideas together. It may be useful to limit the number of ideas that can be put into any one

group so that the groups don't become so large that they become meaningless. Be careful to keep each group limited to one idea or motivation type, do split it down further into sub-groups if necessary. For example, one group might be about 'Cost considerations', with subgroups 'Too expensive' and 'Value concerns.'

3. **Add group headings:** Write titles or headers for each of the groups that you have created. The headings should summarise the overall idea that the statement represents. For example, headings might be things like 'Financial', 'Logistics', or "Process practicality'.

Figure 3: Affinity diagram

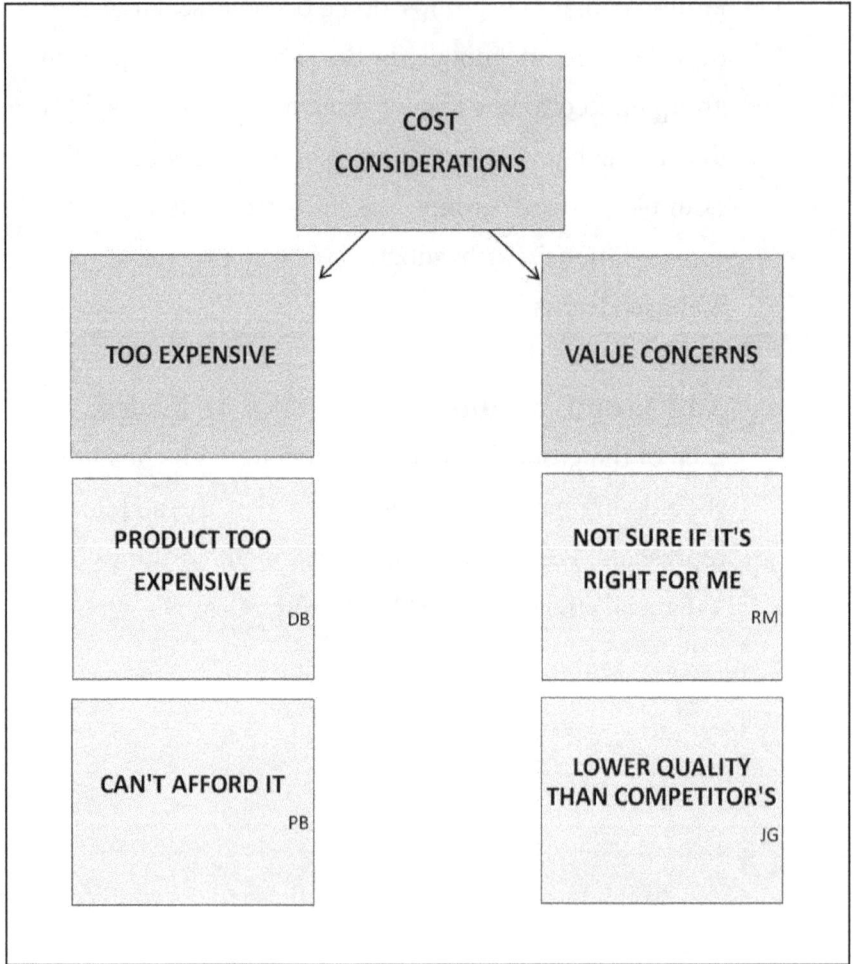

ATTITUDINAL VARIABLES

Once you have created affinity diagrams, you can start to look for patterns of attitudes and behaviours within each of your groupings by positioning each response on a scale. These scales are designed to reveal what we call 'attitudinal variables'.

The numbers or initials you added to the Post-it notes when you created the affinity diagrams will help you to identify which interviewees consistently appear together on the scales. Interviewees with kindred attitudes and behaviours represent one kind of customer, which will later translate to one buyer persona.

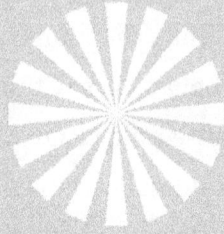

PERSONA ACTION #5

Follow the instructions below to create a scale of attitudinal variables.

1. Take a large sheet of paper or a whiteboard and draw some horizontal lines that will form a series of scales.
2. Next take each group and place the individual points on a variable scale, based on things like:

-   Goals and motivations.
-   Attitudes.
-   Knowledge and expectations.
-   Behaviours.
-   Needs.
-   Brand knowledge or awareness.
-   Product awareness.

Figure 4: Attitudinal variables

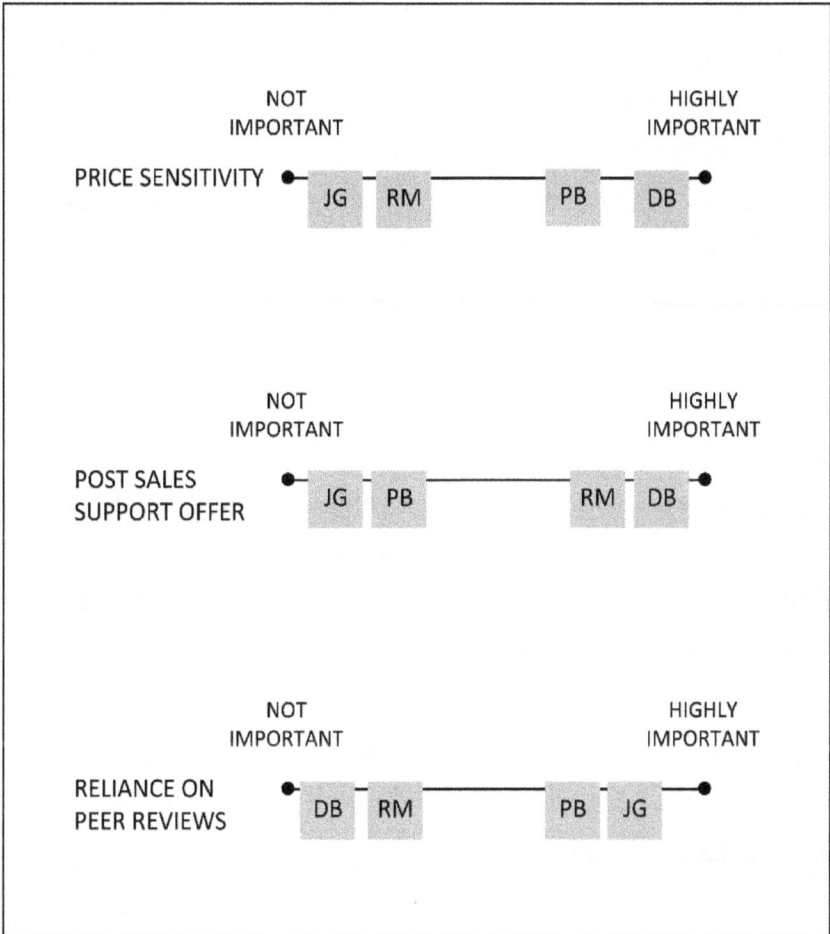

COMPOSING THE PERSONAS

Now that you have created clusters of ideas, you are able to use these groupings to work out which of your interviewees have similar behavioural characteristics.

For example, you might find that, across many of the scales, interviewees #1, #3 and #5 consistently appear together, while #2, #4 and #6 are also positioned closely. These groupings of interviewees will form the basis of your personas.

For each grouping, write a narrative around the common behavioural and attitudinal characteristics, forming a description of a person that embodies this group of interviewees.

Specifically describe motivations and needs and how they drive certain behaviours. Try to keep the narrative relevant in some way to content requirements; it is easy to go off on a tangent and write charming and fluffy descriptions that miss the key points.

Think back to Adele Revella's *Five Rings of Buyer Insight* to help prioritise the characteristics you feature in the personas. Remember that everything you include must be grounded in the data you have collected.

PERSONA ACTION #6

It's time to bring each persona to life by consolidating all of the information we have about our personas. We'll also give them a name and photograph, which will help you to think about the personas as real people and more easily distinguish between them.

First of all, download the persona template on the Content Marketing Coup website, or create your own.

Include the following information for each persona.

1. **Demographics:** Based on the cluster of interviewees that formed the persona, create a demographic profile that most closely represents the group. This should include information like gender, age range, income, location, etc.

2. **Description:** Write a few sentences describing what type of person they are, such as what they are interested in, what they like or dislike and anything

else that usefully characterises this persona and sets it apart from the other personas.

3. **Motivation and drive:** In relation to your product area and content, write a list of the persona's key motivating factors. What makes them buy or not buy? What creates their need to buy? How do they go about finding a solution?

4. **Main enquiries:** Write a list of the personas key enquiries in relation to your product area. You need to take yourself out of the equation; you're not looking for enquiries they may have in relation to your product; you're looking for more general interpretations.

Figure 5: Persona template

PERSONA NAME

Age:	Profession:
Gender:	Salary:
Location:	Education:

BACKGROUND PROFILE:

Lorem ipsum dolor sit amet, adipiscing elit, sed diam nonummy nibh euismod tincidunt ut laoreet dolore magna erat volutpat. Ut wisi enim ad minim.

MOTIVATIONS & GOALS:

- Lorem ipsum dolor sit amet
- Adipiscing lit sed diam nonummy
- Nibh euismod incidunt ut laoreet
- Dolore magna erat lutpat
- Ut wisi enim ad minim

"A one sentence quote that summarises the persona will go here."

BEHAVIOUR:

- Duis autem vel eum molestie consequat, vel illum dolore eu feugiat nulla
- Eodem modo typi in hendrerit in vulputate velit
- Mirum est notare quam litter
- Qui blandit praesent fiant soll omnes in futurum
- Ut wisi enim ad minim lorem ipsum dolor sit amet adipiscin lit sed diam nonummy
- Nibh euismod incidunt ut dolo magna erat lutpat, ut wisi eni ad minim

WHAT I WANT TO KNOW:

- Mirum est notare quam litter
- Qui blandit praesent fiant soll omnes in futurum
- Duis autem vel eum molestie consequat, vel illum dolore eu feugiat nulla
- Eodem modo typi in hendrerit in vulputate velit
- Nibh euismod incidunt ut dolo magna erat lutpat, ut wisi eni ad minim
- Ut wisi enim ad minim lorem ipsum dolor sit amet adipiscin lit sed diam nonummy

5

BUYER'S JOURNEY

*"It is the direction and not the magnitude
which is to be taken into consideration."*

Thomas Paine

To a greater or lesser degree, every customer goes through the
same basic journey before buying a product, it is just that certain
stages take longer for some customers than others. Thoroughly
understanding how different types of customers progress through
this journey will help you to recognise opportunities to influence
(and even speed up) progression at each stage.

By providing valuable content, you can have meaningful
contact with potential customers at all of these stages, but it has to

be the right kind of content. Your task is to recognise what they need and when they need it.

Figure 6: Buyer's Journey

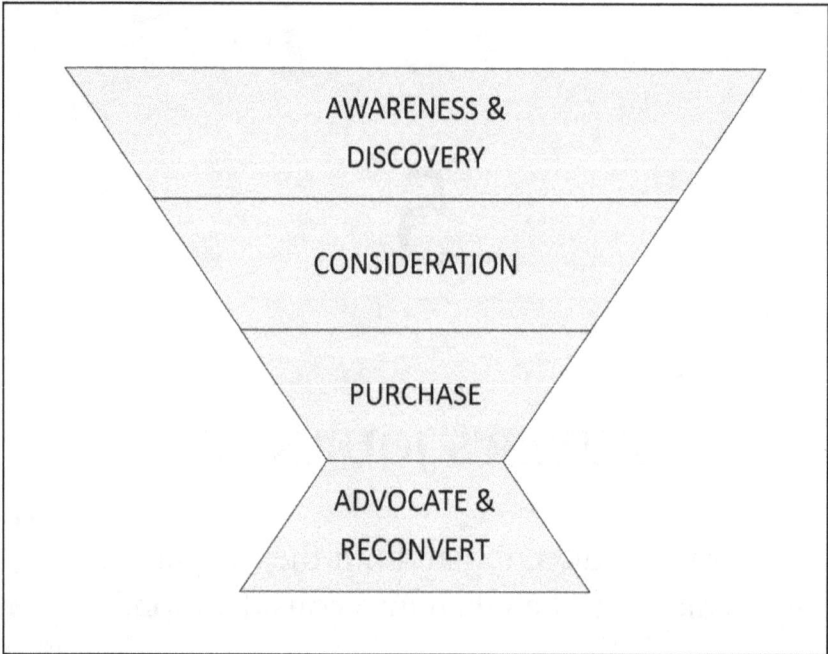

1. AWARENESS & DISCOVERY

AWARENESS

This is the stage of the buyer's journey where some kind of need or desire emerges. The customer probably doesn't know that a solution exists at this point and, more than likely, they will not have heard of your company.

Your aim at this stage is to create awareness of your existence, while demonstrating relevant authority and expertise. Typically, at this point, the customer is looking for lighter content that helps to introduce a new idea or concept. Here, you are aiming to inspire the potential buyer's interest in the topic.

Examples of good 'Awareness and Discovery' stage content include entry-level material that talks around the customer's emerging need or desire, such as:

- Blog posts.
- How-to guides (including articles, videos, etc.).
- Reports and eBooks.
- Diagnostic tools.
- Infographics.
- Whitepapers (mainly for B2B customers).

Your content should include a suggestion about the next step for the buyer. Calls to action at the 'Awareness and Discovery' stage should direct the buyer towards supplementary content within the same stage, or gently direct them towards content within the 'Consideration' stage. Either way, it should encourage them to engage with the content on some level, for example:

- Visit or download related content.
- Leave a comment or ask a question.
- Share the content on social media.
- Subscribe to a newsletter.
- Follow for more information on the topic.

Remember, your aim is to provide *useful* content; there should be no bias towards your products or brand. You are serving to educate the user, not necessarily provide the full solution just yet.

DISCOVERY

This is the most difficult stage of the journey for getting your content discovered by the target audience. The fact the customer is not necessarily informed about their need or desire means they are probably not yet searching for a solution at all.

It is important to search engine optimise your online content with keywords, title tags and URLs that take into account the fact that your audience is unlikely to be familiar with the 'correct' terminology. It's important to use plain English rather than the jargon that more qualified customers might be searching.

You need to do the same for offline content, such as print materials; it is important that you distribute your content in the places that your audience might be looking for solutions, rather than just the places that qualified leads go. It's about being creative with your positioning, as well as using headlines, taglines and text that entices prospects with limited knowledge of the topic. Get into your personas shoes and target the most likely places they will look.

You can find out what terms and phrases your customers are searching with free keyword analysis tool, Wordtracker. *Figure 7* shows popular terms associated with 'content marketing'.

Figure 7: Wordtracker

Keyword	Volume
content marketing	537
content marketing strategy	70
kudani content marketing	42
marketing content	33
salad bar content marketing	27
what is content marketing	25
content marketing magazine	24
min read content marketing	23
content marketing principles	22
content marketing titles	19

Source: Wordtracker © www.wordtracker.com

ATTENTION!

Regardless of type or format, all content should have headlines or titles that clearly communicate its value to the audience at their current stage. The buyer doesn't know exactly what they need yet, so capture their attention by telling them why they should look at your content. Why is it appealing? Who is it useful to? What level is it pitched at?

2. CONSIDERATION

At the 'Consideration' stage, the buyer is aware of a number of potential solutions. They are doing more research than before and feel they are informed enough to start to eliminate some of their earlier considerations.

Your goal at this stage is to help the buyer to find the best solution to their problem, as well as prepare them to evaluate your brand's offering. Ultimately, you are aiming to now start converting your audience into prospects.

Though you will continue to provide enlightening content, you will pitch it at a slightly higher level, with more focus on solution comparisons. At this stage, you're looking to demonstrate the best options and build faith in your brand, *without selling*. Types of valuable content at this stage include:

- Platforms for discussion, such as forums.
- Relevant case studies.
- Customer testimonials.
- Demonstrative videos.
- Tutorials.
- Comparison articles.
- Newsletters and eBooks.
- FAQs.

Your calls to action are going to be similar to those at the 'Discovery' stage, but now you want to encourage customers to engage with you, while continuing to push other supporting content and shuffle the prospect along to the 'Purchase' stage. But, remember, you're still not pushing your audience to buy anything yet.

3. PURCHASE

At the 'Purchase' stage, your audience is ready to select a product or provider and make a purchase.

They will now need to think about the final points that will clinch the decision, such as pricing, practicality and availability of customer support. Therefore, your content should aim to reassure the buyer about your solution.

This is the stage that customers will be most receptive to more traditional marketing tactics, so your content should aim to balance any sales-focussed content and maintain the unbiased voice you have carefully developed up until this point. Content that supports the 'Purchase' stage includes:

- Case studies with a post-sale focus (what are other customers' experiences?).
- Customer-generated testimonials.
- Live in-person events.
- Return on investment forecasts and calculation tools.
- Pricing, package and offer guides.
- Guides about managing any associated post-sale costs.
- User support documentation.
- Functional tools that support the product.
- Discussions online about the product.
- In-depth tutorials.

The calls to action at this stage will be supportive of the sales *process*, rather than the sales *decision*. You will direct people towards special offers, discounts and direct contact with the company.

4. ADVOCATE AND RECONVERT

One of the main aims of brand building is to turn customers into loyal advocates. How can you make sure your customers want to be associated with your products?

At this stage, you want to encourage customers to reach out to other prospects and promote your solution for the greater good. Post-sale, the valuable content that will enrich the experience of customers will prepare them for advocacy and upselling.

USER-GENERATED CONTENT

Nothing persuades customers more than the recommendations of existing customers. Equally, nothing inspires loyalty more than a feeling of community. By encouraging customers to create and share their own content relevant to your product not only empowers existing customers to use their voice to endorse your product, it inspires community among your customers and, crucially, it has authenticity written all over it.

CONSISTENT MESSAGES

The content that you have provided throughout the cycle so far should have helped to establish a consistent, authoritative and trusted voice. A lot of companies fall down by failing to nurture post-sale relationships. You must continue to provide valuable and relevant content that will help you to up-sell and transform your customers into brand advocates.

Given customers trust the opinions of other buyers more than anything a company tells them, you want to encourage them to shout about their positive experiences. At this stage, one of your focuses should be highly-shareable content that rewards your customers for sharing by transferring street cred or authority. Examples of this kind of content include:

- Aspirational or 'showy' content (look at me!).
- Contests and giveaways.
- Games.
- Special offers.
- Hints, tricks and life hacks related to the brand.

SUBSCRIBE OR DIE

It is essential to capitalise on the relationship you have worked so hard to nurture by keeping a communications channel open. If they haven't signed up already, it's important to encourage your customers to subscribe to receive notifications about your post-sale content.

BUYER'S JOURNEY ACTION

Create a map of your own buyer's journey. You can draw it or download the free template on the *Content Marketing Coup* website.

At each stage of the journey, write down the key issues and considerations each of your buyer personas has.

Return to this map each time you're going to create some new content. Think about where this content fits into the journey and how it either supports the buyer at this stage or drives them onward in the journey.

MISSION SUMMARY

Get infatuated with the buyer's journey! Live it and breathe it. Immerse yourself in the customer's world and get to know their struggles and triumphs inside out. What are the key pivotal moments in the journey? Make it your mission to find out where they fall down and how they get back up.

6

CONTENT CALENDAR

"Plans are nothing; planning is everything."

Dwight D Eisenhower

However great your content, it is only effective if it is delivered to the right people, at the right time.

The secret is to create a content delivery plan that both capitalises on critical customer moments, but also adopts an efficient and consistent approach. You'll achieve this with the help of a carefully prepared publishing schedule, which we will call your 'content calendar'.

SELECTING THE RIGHT SYSTEM

Whether it's a paper-based diary or dedicated computer software, you need to have a system in place to manage your content calendar. It doesn't matter what tools you choose, as long as they are appropriate for the scale of your activities.

For content marketing plans where the production process is simple and output volumes are moderate, a basic spreadsheet or Outlook calendar is probably suitable. It's also worth thinking about basic online diaries and organisers, particularly for plans that involve slightly more content production. Personally, I've managed reasonably-sized content schedules quite comfortably using Google Calendar, with automated alerts set up for each piece at key intervals.

For those content marketing strategies that involve high volumes of mixed-media, multi-supplier production, you'll need a more robust management system. There are a variety of options available, including Content Kicks, a web-based system I founded in 2016. This system can be used to help plan and schedule content prior to publication, while also making it easier to manage collaborations between multiple content producers, assign tasks and manage time/budgets.

NOMINATE OWNERSHIP

Quite possibly, your content will be generated by a number of different people within your organisation and maybe even by outsourced content providers. While this approach often bears fruit in the shape of high-quality, rich, varied content, it also means the workflow feed can become fragmented. So where does the buck stop if content isn't flowing consistently? Who will take responsibility? Why not give one person within the company (maybe you) ownership of the content calendar and workflow? If no single person has responsibility, there will be no one to keep you on course.

ALLOCATE PRODUCERS & SOURCES EARLY

For each piece of content in your plan, you will allocate the individual or agency that will produce it. But you must always ensure that production deadlines are agreed with all parties before the item goes into the content calendar. Although you're going to need to switch things around occasionally, you want these switches to be driven by customer need and market opportunities rather than administrative or resourcing issues.

I also find it useful to build advance notices about production deadlines into the calendar, which allows time for producers to be reminded of agreed timescales. It's better to send a reminder early than chase late!

TO COMMIT OR NOT TO COMMIT?

The amount of content you plan to distribute throughout the year should be ambitious, but also achievable. Every item you put into the content calendar is a commitment to publishing on that date, at that time, and you need to respect it.

The best way to ensure you stick to the calendar is to only commit content items if you are confident you have the resources and/or budget required for them to be delivered.

CONTENT CALENDAR ACTION #1

For every piece of content you schedule, you'll attach three key dates. One to make sure it is actually created, one to make sure it gets published at the right time and one to monitor it post-publishing:

1. **Production deadline:** Take into account how much time and resources production of the content will require and set an achievable deadline. Remember to be realistic: stretching is good, but breaking is bad.

2. **Publication date:** Make sure you allow enough time after the production date for it to be checked, reviewed and amended. A lot of people make the mistake of not allowing enough time for this. As a general rule of thumb, I tend to allow at least a third of the time that

was allocated to production.

3. **Review date:** Adding a review date helps to ensure the content isn't just published and forgotten about. Out of date content can be just as damaging to your brand as good content can be rewarding. The review date will depend on the type of content, its content and the subject matter. Are there any events or dates that put the content at risk of being inaccurate or dated?

PLAN FOR THEMES & SERIES

Producing content as part of a theme or series is a great way of getting your teeth into an important topic, while maintaining audience contact over a longer period. Think video or blog series, for example. The great thing about content-in-series is that you're able to build a relationship with the audience over a longer period, while also demonstrating your brand's consistent and reliable principles (if these are your values when it comes to content, it must be the same when it comes to your products, right?). But you can obviously only make this impression if your publishing pattern is actually consistent. For example, maybe you'll publish instalments on the same day, every week.

CONSIDER THE CALENDAR YEAR

It's important that you plan and organise your content publishing around key events, dates, product launches and any sector or regulatory patterns that might apply. How is the buyer's journey affected by these dates?

For example, in the case of a university, the undergraduate applicant's journey is broadly mapped to the academic year and events that are specific to the sector, such as open day seasons, application windows, clearing, etc. As a result, prospects require specific content at certain times of the year.

WHAT ABOUT BUSINESS COMMITMENTS?

Think about your business calendar. How will your resources be affected during busy periods? If you're producing content in-house, it's important you account for the times resources are likely to be stretched thin. For instance, if the annual report or a new product launch is likely to cause bottlenecks, it is best to avoid content blackouts and backlogs by preparing content well in advance.

CONTENT CALENDAR ACTION #2

Think about content that you plan to publish as part of a series. For example, blog posts, articles and video tutorials. Before you start creating anything, try to answer the following:

1. If the series has a limited number of instalments, how many will there be?

2. How often will you publish (think about your audience's needs as well as the resources you'll need to create the content)?

3. Are there any calendar events over the course of the series that will make certain topics more pertinent at specific times?

4. How much lead time can you build in to your production schedule to allow the topics to change or be re-ordered so you can seize market opportunities?

MISSION SUMMARY

Given that 70% of content marketers lack consistency in their strategy (according to Altimeter research), there is a real opportunity to get ahead of your competitors with a well-planned content calendar.

Strong discipline and an acute understanding of the market will be your new best friends. Aim for a well-informed plan that is fluid enough to respond to new opportunities as they arise. But remember, there is a fine balance to strike between commitment to the schedule and pragmatism in your approach.

Respect your content calendar, after all, it is the roadmap towards a more consistent, efficient and resourceful operation.

7

CONTENT TYPES

"Success is not final, failure is not fatal:
it is the courage to continue that counts."

Sir Winston Churchill

Every business has a finite amount of money and resources to spend on marketing, so don't waste any of it by creating content types that won't earn their keep. Choosing between content types will be much easier if you allow your market research, buyer personas and buyer's journey to guide you. But, remember that the best solution might not be the most obvious.

Throw away any assumptions that tie content types to certain content ideas. For instance, just because it's a tutorial, it doesn't mean it has to be a video; just because it's a piece of analysis, it doesn't mean it has to be a whitepaper.

If you want to make a real difference in your customers' world, don't allow your messages to be constrained by archetypal content types.

The content type you choose for each piece should be most appropriate to your audience's requirements, the platform you will publish on and, of course, the action you're aiming to drive as a result of the content. Let's take a closer look at some of your options.

BLOGS

Blogs are the hub of most brands' content marketing activities, partly because their natural structure (heading, main body, lists and links) means they can easily be optimised for search engines.

Regularly posting useful, interesting or entertaining blogs can also help you to get to know your audience better, as well as test out new topics and themes by monitoring interactions and analytics.

Your blog posts should be primarily published to owned channels, such as your website, microsites or dedicated blog sites. Publishing blog posts primarily on rented channels like LinkedIn and blog communities leaves your content at the mercy of third parties, who have the power to change rules around publishing privileges and organic reach.

ORIGINAL DATA & RESEARCH

Reports, data sheets and research studies can be extremely valuable content, particularly in B2B settings. You can either conduct a dedicated study in a targeted area of interest, or you can use data you already have that comes from your market research, customer questionnaires or general business activities.

Depending on whether the depth and volume of research justifies it, you can gear this kind of content for lead generation at the point of access (for example, by requesting contact details). You can then use this to feed more relevant content to the user in the future.

SLIDESHARE PRESENTATIONS

Using SlideShare, you can create and share presentations, infographics, documents, videos, PDFs, and webinars. Your content can then easily be disseminated across social media and embedded within websites and blogs. This is particularly good for reusing existing company presentations and materials.

GUIDES & MANUALS

Creating user guides and manuals is a great way of using in-house expertise to provide value to your target customers. Your guides don't just have to focus on how to use your products and services; they can also cover things like improving efficiency, making the most of specific features and maximising product lifespan. You can even go beyond your products and services and create guides that deal with customer 'pain points' that don't directly relate to your commercial offering.

WHITE PAPERS

In publishing a white paper, you have an opportunity to offer an authoritative perspective on specific issues in a report format. The aim of your white paper should be to help customers to understand key issues, solve a problem, or make a decision.

DATA SHEETS

Data sheets, otherwise known as technical summaries or specifications, are documents that summarise the performance and technical characteristics of services and products (such as machines and components). Publishing this kind of content alongside your products and services can help your customers to make more informed decisions throughout the buyer's journey, from the 'Purchase' to 'Advocate and Reconvert' stages.

LISTS

People love lists. How many times have you read things like *"The Top 100 X"* or *"7 reasons to Y"*? If you target your customers effectively, this kind of content can be extremely engaging and shareable, yet it doesn't always involve a huge investment in time, resources or skills. If you were a travel company, how difficult would it be for you to produce a list of your top 10 recommended holiday destinations?

LINK PAGES

Similarly to list pages, link pages pull together resources from around the internet (which can be ours or third-party) and display them in one place as a directory.

Production-wise, the main investment will be time for research and long-term maintenance of external links (which tend to move or break over time). If you work the maintenance into your content calendar, you can more easily mitigate the risk of broken links.

WEBINARS

Online seminars are a great way to provide valuable content in the form of live training, workshops, lectures and consultations. Webinar services enable real-time point-to-point communications and multicast communications from one sender to many receivers. They offer data streams of text-based messages, voice and video chat to be shared simultaneously, across the globe.

There are a number of free and paid webinar services, including Click Webinar and Any Meeting.

EBOOKS

One of the best ways you can elevate your authority and credibility in your field is to publish an eBook. It is also one of the best ways to reach large volumes of the target audience, but your success will ultimately depend on the production quality and value of your content.

You can publish eBooks as downloads on your website, or make them accessible for Kindle and e-reader devices, using services such as Create Space and Book Baby.

VIDEOS

Whether your content is informative, entertaining or thought provoking, video is one of the most popular and versatile content types you can choose. In terms of reach and shareability, it can offer substantial return on investment when targeted and amplified appropriately.

When it comes to publishing, there is a range of paid and free distribution channels that allow you to embed videos within websites and also enable them to be shared easily across social media channels. As a starting point, take a look at YouTube, Vimeo and uploads direct to Facebook.

SCREENCASTS

Also known as video screen captures, screencasts are digital recordings of computer screen outputs and usually include audio narration and text annotations. They are ideal for educational uses, including software presentations, tutorials and troubleshooting guides.

There is a range of free and paid software packages you can use to create screencasts easily. Start by looking at Cam Studio and Screencast-O-Matic.

LIVE-STREAMING VIDEO

A great way of engaging audiences with real-time content is live-streaming video. This can be used effectively for coverage of things like round-table discussions, events and presentations. Incorporate this with live audience participation, such as real-time questions and answers, and you have a truly real-time content experience.

Take a look at YouTube's live streaming service and Meerkat.

PODCASTS

Podcasts are a great way of getting your content to target customers in an easily accessible format, which they can listen to while on the move. They tend to work best as part of a series, or at least as a consistent flow of episodes. The great thing about podcasts is they can be audio versions of written content or they can be specially produced for audio. They work great in radio programme format for discussions and interviews.

A good quality microphone and suitable recording location are paramount considerations for media quality, but it need not cost the earth. A decent USB condenser microphone can be sought from as little as $80.

INFOGRAPHICS

Infographics are great for conveying information in an easy-to-digest format with a mixture of graphics and text. Whether you're displaying processes, timelines or complex data you can use infographics to display the information simply and clearly, with easy emphasis on trends and patterns. Educational and great for social sharing, infographics can be used repeatedly by you and by other content curators.

To create an infographic, you can either use the services of a graphic designer or use an online tool like Infogram or Piktochart.

COMICS & CARTOON STRIPS

Useful when making both simple and complex points, comic strips and cartoons are visually appealing, easy to follow and can be used to make points quickly. They can be used to demonstrate and simplify processes, explain or emphasise theories, and create humorous interpretations that your audience can identify with. If well produced, cartoons can be highly engaging and extremely sharable online.

There are a number of free and subscription online programmes that can be used to create and share this kind of content in a variety of styles, with little design experience required. Try Pixton or Go Animate.

MEMES

Often used to represent concepts, catchphrases or pieces of media, memes use images, videos, hyperlinks, hashtags and/or pieces of text. They are very short, humorous in nature and built for sharing across social networks.

Memes are simple to make with basic editing software, but there are also a number of websites and apps that can be used, including Imgflip and Meme Generator.

CASE STUDIES

Case studies are a great way of showing off examples of your brand at its best, along with demonstrating real-life examples of service excellence. Rather than telling your audience how great you are, you are showing them with examples they can relate to.

INTERVIEWS

Interviews with influencers, industry experts, customers and even staff within your own company can prove to be very engaging content. You can present this content in a range of formats, including copy, audio, video and in-person events.

IN-PERSON EVENTS

Great for pulling in a captive audience, hosting in-person events, such as conferences and workshops, can be particularly engaging for customers.

The keys to a successful event are a well-targeted audience, engaging promotional hooks (including topics and guest speakers) and content that is highly-relevant to the audience.

DOWNLOADABLE TEMPLATES

Creating usable templates that customers can use to complete or structure tasks is a simple and effective way of offering value. Whether it is an excel spreadsheet for bookkeeping or a dress making pattern, this type of content enables you to share existing internal resources, materials or documentation to provide value that your customers will use time and time again.

FREE STOCK

Perhaps you have a whole bank of photography or video that your target customers would find useful. By creating a database of free photography or video you can deliver value in the form of free, re-usable stock media. Take a look at free image website, Unsplash, for inspiration.

EMAILS

You're probably already using emails to deliver marketing messages to your target customers, but you can also use this channel to deliver valuable content to your audience in the same way. You can either embed the content into email templates or link to content that lives elsewhere.

NEWS ARTICLES

Publishing new articles is a great way of demonstrating that your finger is on the pulse of your industry. By producing and/or curating relevant news articles on the topics that matter to your customers, you can take a step towards being the go-to source for news in your field. Before you commit to publishing news, you need to consider how this fits in with your long-term plan. As the name suggests, news will need to be published regularly at consistent intervals.

You can either create your own online or offline newsletter, or use an online platform, such as Paper.li or The Tweeted Times.

THIRD-PARTY PRODUCT REVIEWS

Reviewing products and services that are relevant to your target audience can help to demonstrate your specialist expertise. But in order for your reviews to be valuable, they must be neutral and objective. For this reason, avoid reviewing products you have a commercial interest in.

On the other hand, feel free to share or republish the best and most interesting third-party reviews of your own products or services if your customers will find them useful.

CONTENT COMPETITIONS

By developing content competitions, you can attract and engage specific customer segments, build your brand profile and develop long-term relationships with your audience. Not least, they also generate a whole bank of customer-generated content.

There is a range of platforms you can use to both run the competitions and accept the entries, including social media channels (Instagram and Facebook are particularly popular platforms for competitions), email communications and, of course, via your website.

Remember to include rules, terms and conditions, closing date and details of any prizes on offer.

MOBILE APPS

Mobile apps are natural born engagement tools and enable a participatory element to your content that isn't always functionally or logistically possible on other platforms.

By creating a mobile app, you can send a regular stream of valuable content straight to the hands of your target audience in a highly-targeted way. You know exactly who the user is and how they are interacting with your content. You can use this information to customise the brand experience for each customer, delivering truly valuable content at all of the crucial times.

BRANDED MICROSITES

By creating a branded microsite, you can pull together all of the content you have created for a specific theme and present it in one place under a dedicated brand. Not only does this provide you with a platform for promoting and showcasing niche content, you're able to create a more objective magazine-style feel to the package.

PRINT MAGAZINES

Though you're deep into the digital age, there is certainly still a welcome place for print magazines and pamphlets. Depending on your niche and the customers you're targeting, a print magazine might be a smart way to tap into your audience. Look at the continued success of print publications like *The Furrow* magazine, *LEGO Club* and *BenchMark Magazine*.

TV & RADIO SHOWS

While this might seem like a far-fetched idea on the face of it, many businesses and individuals build their public profiles by appearing on TV and radio shows. Whether you're aiming to star in your own network TV show like *Million Dollar Listing*, or you want to be the local radio station's go-to expert on your specialist topic, TV and radio appearance can elevate your authority faster than any other medium.

Look out for media opportunities advertised in the press, but also get in touch with TV and radio companies to offer your services as expert commentators. At the same time, get on the media radar by actively participating in relevant radio phone-ins and TV debates.

TV and radio are areas that niche targeting is less important in the grand scheme. In this case, the bigger the platform, the more celebrated your expertise.

BOOK REVIEWS

Even if you don't have the time or the resources to produce your own print book or eBook, you can still dip your toe into the world of publishing by writing book reviews. Writing a critical review of a book can demonstrate your expertise and authority in the field, while also proving you're up to date with current literature in the field.

Bear in mind that publishing your review on a bookstore website (such as Amazon) will restrict you in terms of copy length and structure, as well as reach or virality. Instead, try publishing it somewhere that offers more control, such as your own website, blog or YouTube.

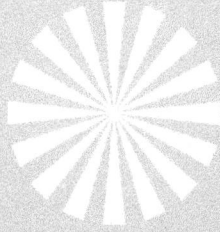

CONTENT TYPES ACTION

Before you create any new content, ask yourself following questions to help decide on the most suitable format.

1. Is the content intended to help, educate or entertain your audience?
2. How will the content most easily be accessed by the audience for its intended purpose (e.g. if the content is a tutorial, would a video or audio format allow the user to perform a task while using the content)?
3. What platforms or channels does your target audience primarily use to access this kind of content (e.g. Facebook, blog sites, books)?
4. Which of the audience's favourite content types fit best with your content production capabilities?
5. How important is the content to the buyer's journey in relation to the production cost?

9

CONTENT CURATION

*"Building up a comradeship is the
greatest of all feats."*

Edmund Hillary

Republishing other people's content is a great way to use their
voice and influence to help bolster your messages, deliver value to
your customers and drive forward your strategy by supporting
specific objectives. The practice, known as *content curation* can not
only add strength and credibility to your messages by
demonstrating objectivity, it also means you're able to provide your
audience with great quality content without having to create it all
yourself.

By sifting, sorting and republishing the best of the information available in your category, you're able to position yourself as a thought leader in your field. The fact you're making qualified editorial decisions about other people's content helps to demonstrate your knowledge in the field. Plus, from your audience's point of view, you are saving them time by finding, filtering and organising content that they want to see.

In fact, from a practical point of view, content curation can help you to beat the top challenges you face as a content marketer, including saving time and money and ensuring a steady flow of engaging multi-format content.

Figure 8: Top five cited content marketing challenges

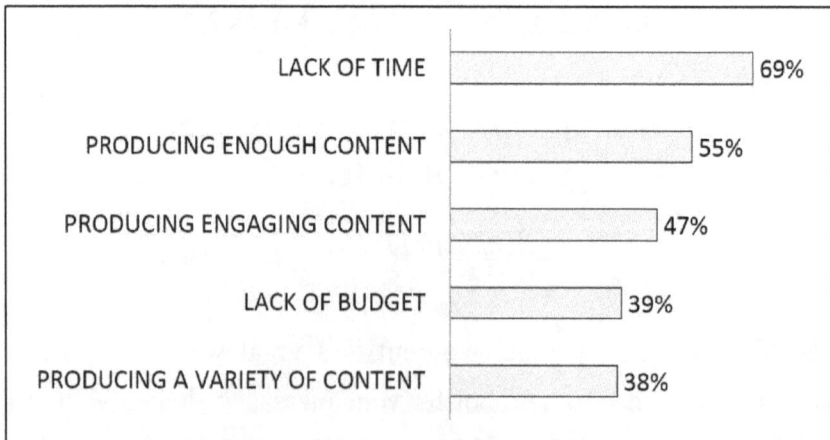

Data source: 2014 B2B Content Marketing Trends North America © Content Marketing Institute/Marketing Profs

Although the advantages of effective content curation are clear, there are a number of things you need to consider in order to protect your brand and mitigate some of the risks that come with using other people's content.

EDITORIAL JUDGEMENT

Too many content marketers go crazy with curation because they see it as an easy and cost-effective way to flood their market with content. There are a number of tools available that make it very easy to gather and republish content from around the internet (we will look at tools later), but selecting the right content to publish requires skill and close consideration of your objectives.

If you publish content that isn't perfectly in tune with your target audience and your objectives, you risk portraying your brand as out of touch and irrelevant. Content with the wrong focus will only dilute your message and distract your audience from the really valuable stuff in your portfolio.

The same principles you use to make editorial judgements when you're creating content also apply to the curation process. Is the content highly-relevant to your target customers? How does the content help support the buyer's journey? What particular goals or objectives does it support?

LISTEN, WATCH, READ

You need to cast your net as widely as possible in order to find the best content relevant to your target audience and objectives. There are a number of tools that can alert you to content that is being published within your areas of interest, including:

- Curata gathers topic-specific content from hundreds of thousands of sources across the internet. With a high degree of tailoring, the system learns and dynamically adapts to content preferences and easily integrates with CMS (content management systems), social and email marketing platforms. This is the heavyweight curator's choice, with 'Professional' and 'Enterprise' monthly pricing options.

- ScoopIt uses big data semantic technology to scour 20 million web pages each day for high-quality, relevant content. This system comes with the Smart Calendar to help plan and manage the publishing process. There are a range of packages from a free taster option to an enterprise-level 'content director' plan.

- Swayy helps you to discover and reuse engaging content across social media. With a built-in analytics platform, the system is designed to suggest the most effective content for growing your community. Prices range from a free basic account to a 100 dashboard agency-level plan.

- Feedley compiles news feeds from a wide range of sources and includes an easy customisation and publishing dashboard. The generous basic package is free with premium upgrades to Pro and Team versions available.

- TrapIt uses advanced artificial intelligence and machine learning to create real-time content collections, called 'traps,' The system, which allows drill-down by location and media type, can publish content to websites, social media and mobile applications. A free demo version is available upon request.

SUPPORTING THEMES

Think of your curated material as nominees for Best Supporting Actor, while your own content takes the leading roles. You need to ensure that everything you collect fits in with your broader themes of focus. How can third-party content create a more rounded picture and contribute to shaping your topics? If it's not obvious how the content supports your specific messages, you probably shouldn't be publishing it.

REINFORCE YOUR VOICE

Let's step outside of your own world for a moment and remember that your audience probably isn't interested in your brand per se. They are interested in meeting some kind of need and nothing more.

The problem is, everything you produce yourself is quietly whispering "me, me, me". Naturally, your content is all about *your* advice and *your* perspective, but too much of your own messaging without support from objective third parties starts to give your content a narcissistic feel.

You can balance your "me, me, me" voice by using third-party content to demonstrate support for the content you are putting out. You should look for content that you can use to validate and reinforce your own voice.

GO FOR INFLUENCERS

Have you the heard the expression "You are the company you keep"? It is certainly true that customers will judge you against the people you're associated with. Just think about the millions of dollars companies pay to be endorsed by celebrities and sport personalities.

By curating the content of key influencers in your field, you can link your brand with the key individuals and organisations your customers care about. Publishing influencer content not only demonstrates positive affinities, it also allows you to borrow some of their authority.

CREATE A BUZZ

Curation can help you to highlight the discussions people are having about the quieter topic areas you're interested in. You won't whip up much interest in a new niche area if you're the only people talking about it. Let's pull all existing activity together from a variety of sources and present it together. This can reinforce the importance of the topic and attract more attention to it, creating a niche topical buzz.

To add some more credibility to the topic you want to highlight, it is a good idea to pepper it with content from contributors that don't have a commercial interest in the field, such as commentators and independent bloggers.

FIND HARMONIOUS AGENDAS

By identifying publishers that you can have a mutually beneficial relationship with, you can create content partnerships with other brands to bolster your provision. This reduces your resourcing requirements and potentially increases your reach by exposing your content to their audience.

But, remember, regardless of any content sharing deal, all of the same rules apply to editorial decisions; you will only curate content that is appropriate quality and most relevant to your audience.

PLUGGING GAPS

What are the gaps in your expertise or resources that prevent you from creating certain types of content? By curating content that specifically fits into areas you need to prop up, you can provide your target customers with everything they could possibly need.

As well as adding value, your audience will begin to recognise you as a source of objective content on the hot topics. You want to become the go-to source for carefully filtered content.

SUPPORTING SNIPPETS

How can you use snippets of other people's content to support your created content? Bolstering your created content with occasional gems of curated material will save you time and strengthen your arguments.

LEGAL CONSIDERATIONS

Whenever you're using someone else's content within your own work, there are potential legal risks.

Pawan Deshpande, Founder and CEO of Curata, explains: "Fair-use and curation of other people's content becomes an issue when it's not handled properly because the interest of the curator and the publisher overlap significantly. They both want a piece of the same pie: site traffic, increased SEO and visitor retention.

"When the curation is done wrong, the curator's interests are served but the publisher sees no benefit. But if it's done properly, in a symbiotic manner that makes it a win-win, curation can serve the interest of the publisher, and curator, and ultimately the audience."

Figure 9: Publisher and creator overlap

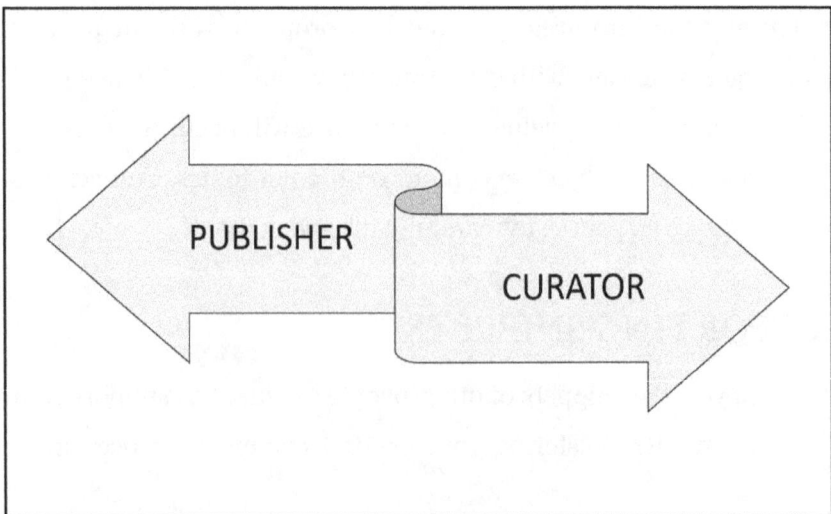

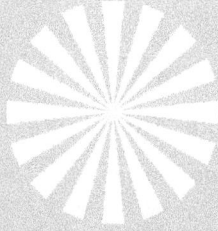

CURATION ACTION

Before publishing any curated content, sense-check your decisions by running the following checks.

1. You have only reproduced a portion of the content; enough to bolster your message and no more.
2. You haven't curated the majority of your total curated output from the same source.
3. You have clearly identified the source and author of the content.
4. You have linked to the original source, where possible.
5. You have made it clear why you are using the content (i.e. to help introduce and contextualise a point).

THE RIGHT MIX

There is a lot of debate around how much of your content should be created versus curated. Some businesses run with 80-100% curated, while others don't curate content at all. There is no one-size-fits-all approach or ideal recipe for success. The ideal ratio for use will depend on the market and sector (including customer needs), your resources (including the size of your business) and your objectives. What do you need to do in order to drive you forward towards the big aim? In all cases, you need to make sure all of your content is effectively moving customers through the buyer's journey.

MISSION SUMMARY

At times, your efforts to secure a place at the top of your market will feel like a bloody battle. Yet, the biggest challenges you face won't always come in the form of direct hits from business rivals. The weakest elements of your own offering, like gaps in expertise and resources, could seriously affect your credibility on certain topics. Occasionally, you're going to need to call in some back-up.

These reinforcements may come in the form of third-party content, carefully curated to bolster these weaker areas. By making smart editorial decisions, you can sort and contextualise valuable content on behalf of your audience. In this case, the value comes in the form of the content package you have created rather than the component pieces.

You can ramp up your clout by linking in with publishers to develop a mutually beneficial relationship. To paraphrase Lyndon B. Johnson, it is better to have certain people inside your tent "spitting" out than outside your tent "spitting" in.

Don't wait for shots to be fired before you identify where your back up is coming from.

10

REAL-TIME PUBLISHING

*"The opportunity is often
lost by deliberating."*

Publilius Syrus

You can react to real-time developments in your market and seize time-limited opportunities by publishing certain types of content on-the-fly.

Reacting and adapting to the audience's world can make your voice more relevant and dynamic, but it can be a risky tactic, so you need to get it right.

IDENTIFY KEY CONVERSATIONS

What are the topics, issues and discussions you want your brand to be associated with? They might be conversations people are already having, or they might be new ones that you're anticipating. Think about how you can valuably contribute to and fuel these conversations early on. How will this content help to boost your voice among the target audience?

LISTEN UP

You can monitor the use of keywords and phrases related to the topics and conversations you are interested in. The best way is to use social media monitoring tools and online keyword scrapers to sift through blogs (including blog comments), news articles and other user-contributed content. There are a large amount of systems available to help with monitoring:

- For social media monitoring, my favourite system is Radian6. With huge data depths, this system scours the internet and highlights virtually every relevant conversation happening right now across the social web.

- Services like BrandWatch dashboard complex keyword searches across social platforms and beyond, with a high degree of filtering. Like Radian6, this is a paid option, but well worth considering if budget allows.

- The best of the free systems is probably Hootsuite, which enables you to identify the words and phrases you're interested in across various social channels, all displayed in a series of real-time feeds.

- Google Alerts is a great free service that allows you to identify keywords and phrases and get real-time alerts when they appear in news and other online publications. There is also a special setting to include results from social media sites.

PIVOT AND ADAPT CONTENT

It is important that you are ready to adapt to the market challenges and opportunities whenever necessary. Don't be afraid to bring scheduled content forward in the content calendar if it is particularly relevant to a current topic. Market need always trumps the schedule.

The same goes for archived and live content. If there is an opportunity to bring it back to prominence or reinvent it, go ahead and adapt, refocus, or republish. But be careful not to crowbar content into tenuously linked topics, as the lack of relevance will be obvious and will only devalue your voice.

PREPARING FOR INVASION

It is best to have a bank of content in reserve, specifically organised into the conversations you're interested in. When the big, important conversations are raging, you'll be armed and ready to contribute rich and valuable content.

INDIVIDUAL TARGETING

You have already discussed how important key market influencers are. While it is crucial that you listen to how they are using their dominant voices, you must remember that every single member of your audience has the potential to influence others.

Some of the biggest companies in the world, including Philips, take the time to respond and deliver bespoke content to audiences of just one person. There is no engagement like a one-to-one engagement.

Creating ad hoc content for individual customers might sound like a great deal of work, but it shouldn't actually be an indiscriminate process. In reality, it is more about responding to individual customers in a very personal way with content that will also appeal to the rest of the audience segment.

ADD VALUE OR GO HOME

Although you need to look for content marketing opportunities around the hot topics you're interested in, you don't need to interact with every single conversation and related sub-topic. Only get involved with hot topics that are relevant to your buyer personas and that you're able to add value to.

DON'T KILL CONVERSATIONS

If you see conversations on websites, social media, blogs and forums that you want to get involved with, it's important that you keep your contributions appropriate and highly-relevant. You want to position yourself as part of the community, almost like friends sharing useful information. But, bear in mind that nobody likes that friend who won't let anyone else speak; you can be that clever, understanding and helpful friend instead.

Remember, you are not telling people where to go next or what to do, you're just going with the flow of the conversation and helping with content where it might be useful. Avoid spammy interruptions!

CREATING IN REAL-TIME

Sometimes an opportunity will arise that calls for content to be created from scratch. The scope for pay-off will be more risky because there just won't be time to follow all of the usual planning and development processes.

REAL-TIME ACTION

Before creating anything on-the-fly, answer the following questions.

1. How will the content specifically contribute to your big aim, goals or objectives?
2. Will the topic still be 'hot' by the time it is ready to publish?
3. Are there any legal considerations associated with publishing the content right now?
4. Is the situation really time-limited?

MISSION SUMMARY

How committed are you to giving your customers what they need? Make it the reason for your entire existence and dedicate your time to focussing on enriching their lives with your content and, believe me, your customers will quickly notice. The more you understand them and respond to their evolving needs, the more chance you will have of earning a place in their lives.

For me, it's about heightening empathy by listening to customers' rants and sharing their joys. If you aren't watching, listening and relating to customers, they will quickly realise you are speaking *at* them, not *with* them.

Go and give it your all to position yourself as that brand that listens to customers and responds with value.

11

IDEA DEVELOPMENT

"No matter what people tell you,
words and ideas can change the world."

Robin Williams

The key to nurturing the best content ideas is knowing your target audience inside out.

It's only by thinking about their needs and desires, in the context of the buyer's journey, that you'll be able to tell the difference between good and bad ideas.

SWEET SPOTS

There is a wonderful point where your specialist knowledge and expertise intersects with specific customers' interests. This is called the 'sweet spot' because targeting that area will usually yield maximum returns.

Figure 10: The sweet spot

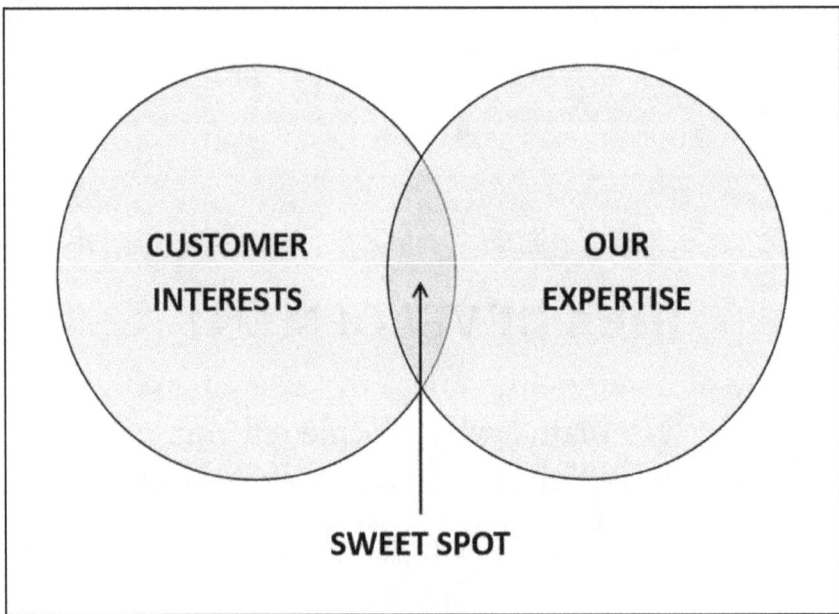

Whenever you're thinking about content ideas, you need to consider how you can use your existing cache of expertise to drill into specific customer interests.

Content that falls within the sweet spot will naturally be easiest for you to create and will also appeal to the biggest portion of your target audience. Additionally, because it's your area of expertise, it's probably also the best authority-building content you're ever likely to create.

That said, if you're looking to engage potential audience segments that aren't currently anywhere near your sales funnel, this content isn't going to touch them. To lasso future prospects early, you need to also think outside of your comfort zone.

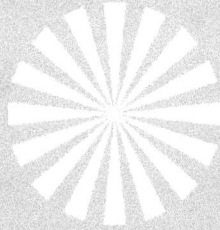

IDEA ACTION #1

Where is your sweet spot? Answer the following questions:

- How does your expertise address issues your audience cares about most?
- Which of your audience's priorities match your specialist subjects?
- What knowledge does your audience crave that you have in abundance?
- Which of your audience's dreams could you most easily make come true?

THINK BEYOND THE PRODUCT

If you can set your brand and products to one side for a moment, you can think about the bigger picture for your personas. What does their world look like? What are the things they care about? What are they doing with their lives right now?

Jay Baer, founder of Convince and Convert, talks a lot about "marketing sideways", which is basically content marketing that is inherently useful, but is not about brand or product. This approach, according to Jay, "transcends the transaction, and creates awareness for your brand at the top of the funnel – among potential customers that otherwise might not be introduced to your company and its offerings".

You need to think about content that will link you up with future prospects that you would struggle to touch with brand or product-related content. How can you capture their attention and interest? How can you establish a relationship that will eventually lead them on to the buyer's journey?

For inspiration, look at Red Bull's focus on extreme sports and music media. This content isn't linked to the company's product at all, but it serves the brand by developing the right image among the target audience. How could this approach work for us?

PAIN POINTS

One of the best ways to attract your target audience is by appealing to their 'pain points'. You can do this by using your content to address (or even solve) specific problems, questions and direct needs.

Not only does this kind of content demonstrate relevant expertise, it also touches your target audience at a pivotal moment in the journey. It's no secret that buyers experiencing issues or 'pain' are most motivated to seek a new solution or switch brands. You can tap into that opportunity.

You need to think about content ideas that address these pain points, but equally consider how important this kind of content can be to the 'Awareness and Discovery' stage of the buyer's journey. What can you do to drive the buyer forward at this early stage? Remember, the people experiencing these pain points will be more open to a new solution, so you need to make the most of your calls to action. How can you use content to form part of a chain that leads potential customers onto the buyer's journey?

IDEA ACTION #2

Identify your customers' pain points. Consider all of the behavioural information you have gathered (your *research*, the *buyer's journey* and your *buyer personas*) and answer the following questions:

- What are the main challenges your customers face?
- What are their perceived barriers to progress?
- Which issues and frustrations matter to them most?
- What do they most want to change or improve?
- What are their biggest fears?

EARLY BIRD ON TRENDS

The smartest content marketers make their efforts more efficient by monitoring search trends and forecast surges in activity.

Analysing web search trends can help you to see what content your target demographic is searching for now, as well as what they are likely to be looking for in the future.

When you used Google Trends as part of your research, what emerging hot topics did you identify?

KEYWORD INSPIRATION

You can get a more detailed picture of search volume for certain keywords using tools like Google Keyword Planner. This reveals more information about the most common keywords for specific search topics, related phrases, monthly search volume and how much competition they carry. All of this information can help you to work out what the most popular topics are, as well as which terms your competitors are interested in.

As an example, the following screenshot shows results returned for a search on 'virtual reality games':

Figure 11: Google Adwords

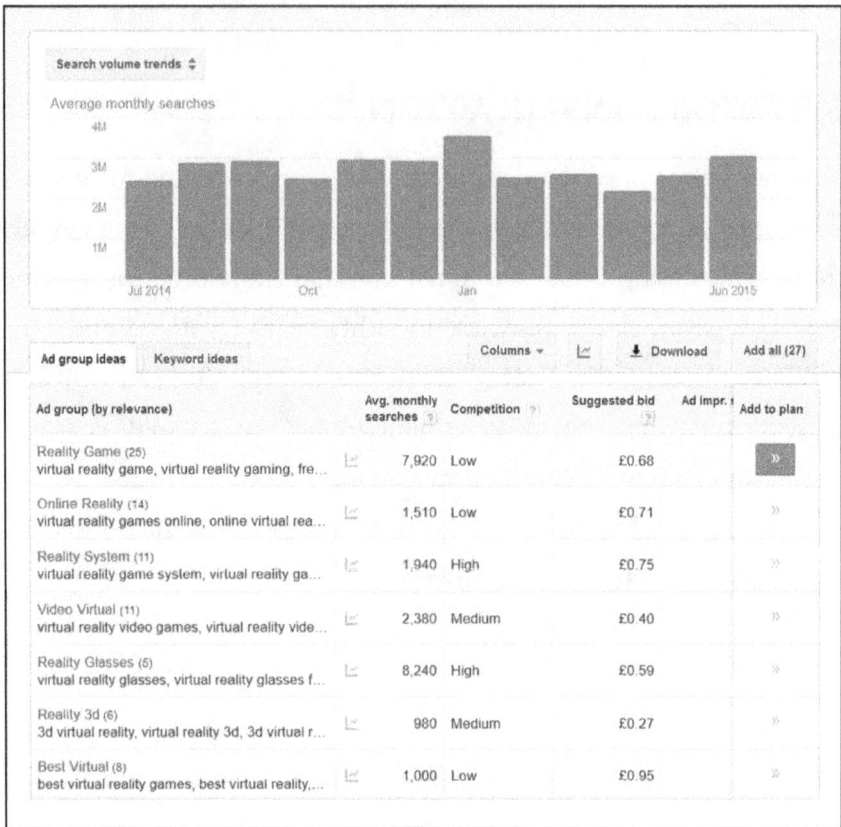

Search volume trends ⇕				

Average monthly searches

Ad group ideas	Keyword ideas			Columns ▾	〜	⬇ Download	Add all (27)
Ad group (by relevance)		**Avg. monthly searches**	**Competition**		**Suggested bid**	**Ad impr.**	**Add to plan**
Reality Game (25) virtual reality game, virtual reality gaming, fre...		7,920	Low		£0.68		»
Online Reality (14) virtual reality games online, online virtual rea...		1,510	Low		£0.71		»
Reality System (11) virtual reality game system, virtual reality ga...		1,940	High		£0.75		»
Video Virtual (11) virtual reality video games, virtual reality vide...		2,380	Medium		£0.40		»
Reality Glasses (5) virtual reality glasses, virtual reality glasses f...		8,240	High		£0.59		»
Reality 3d (6) 3d virtual reality, virtual reality 3d, 3d virtual r...		980	Medium		£0.27		»
Best Virtual (8) best virtual reality games, best virtual reality,...		1,000	Low		£0.95		»

Source: Google AdWords © adwords.google.com

Once you have identified hot keywords, you can use them to inspire content ideas. Identifying the most searched-for terms in a particular field, for a particular demographic, will help you to keep your ideas in the most relevant contexts and maximise your engagement potential.

THE BEATING PULSE

You can keep up to date with what people are talking about right now using websites like Digg and Delicious, which identify hot topics in blog posts, articles and videos across the internet.

What content can you create that fits in with the conversations your target audience is having online? Do you have anything useful to bring to the table?

KNOWLEDGE GAPS

There is a difference between customers not being interested in something because they don't care and them not being interested because they don't have enough knowledge or awareness of the topic.

You have an opportunity to grow your market by qualifying future prospects through informative content that highlights and fills certain knowledge gaps. What content can you create to help your audience to better understand these topics and ultimately channel them into your buyer's journey?

What are the most common customer enquiries about your products and services? What are the most prevalent misconceptions in the product area? You can supplement any internal data you can gather by using websites like Quora and Ask MetaFilter, which provide huge databases of user-generated questions and answers. This research will also help you to identify the type of language your audience is using to describe their knowledge gaps. Mirroring this language in your content not only creates kinship between your brand and the customer, but also helps to make your content more search friendly.

THINK AMPLIFICATION

When you're thinking about content ideas, let's bear in mind how you might amplify the finished product. In other words, how could you construct or present the content to maximise its reach across social media, search engines and content vending sites?

VIRAL POWER UP

Whether or not something has 'gone viral' depends on the size of the specific target market. For us, you might consider a piece of content aimed at a niche group of 1000 people to have gone viral if 800 of the target group have shared or interacted with it. You should consider the following questions when considering the viral potential of your ideas (you don't need to tick every box, but you should aim for at least one):

1. Is the content something people will want to associate themselves with? People are highly conscious of how they are perceived on social media, so if the content doesn't fit in with what I call the audience's 'virtual identity', it won't get shared widely.

2. Is the content remarkable? Ok, you all come across things that are useful, funny or just interesting, but you don't bang on to your friends about all of them. The audience will only share content that is remarkable in some way. If your content idea isn't remarkable, you'll struggle to cast it out very far.

3. Will you interest key influencers? As you discussed earlier, key influencers in your field can catapult your content to large portions of your target audiences. If your content idea appeals to the influencers, it has more chance of being well amplified across their networks.

ACTIONABILITY

It is important that you never forget that every piece of content needs to *do* something for you in some way; it has to perform an *action*. For instance, does it drive your audience to the next stage in the journey, encourage them to use another piece of your content or encourage them to sign up to a mailing list?

CROWD SOURCE IDEAS

Whatever their role, every member of staff within your company has a unique perspective on your brand and customers. You can ask them to put forward content ideas that will help, interest or inspire new and existing customers.

When the ideas are in, you can filter them according to their relevance to buyer personas, the buyer's journey and your big aims.

LOOK AT EXISTING CONTENT STOCK

For a moment, imagine you work for a big movie studio and you're looking for the next big blockbuster. Naturally, you review the most successful movies in the studio's portfolio and wonder how you can recreate those magic, super-successful formulas. Finally, you jump out of the canvas chair and squeal: "I've got it! A sequel!"

Of course, sequels, prequels and remakes of successful movies are usually sure fire cash cows for the studios. After all, there is an existing audience base eagerly waiting for more of the story. As content marketers, how can you do the same? Is there any content you can squeeze a little bit more action out of? Can you add anything to existing content to tell more of the story? Can you 'remake' any of your content to make it better?

Now take another look at your content inventory and audit database and concentrate on the most popular pieces of content. Where are the prequel, sequel and remake opportunities?

SIZE MATTERS

According to research by Static Brain, only 4% of page views hold users' attention for 10 minutes or more. In response, almost 60% of marketers create new 'snackable' versions of existing assets, according to LookBookHQ.

What new content or rehashed existing content can you publish that's quick and easy for your audience to consume?

STEAL INSPIRATION

Although you'll certainly never copy anyone else's work, you should definitely take inspiration from the best content ideas out there. If you find there's a particular piece of content that's being shared, discussed or downloaded widely by your target audience, why not take a closer look at it? Why is it so popular? How could your own version improve this idea?

Coming up with your own unique take on an existing idea isn't as simple as it sounds. You need to make sure your content offers something different, or additional, to the existing content. Duplicating someone else's content is unethical and will do nothing but weaken your message (and your reputation!).

PLATFORMS AND CHANNELS

It's important to frame new content ideas within the channels that your existing customers and prospects are using. There's no point investing time and money to develop content that is not deliverable within the most suitable platforms or channels. What did your research tell you about the platforms and channels that your existing and potential customers are using most?

MISSION SUMMARY

There are companies out there right now that are stealing your customers' attention. Every second of every day, someone, somewhere is creating content that is designed to distract your audience away from your brand. What are you going to do about it?

There are two options: you can either allow your content competitors to take the lead and simply react to their ideas, or you can take a revolutionary stance and beat a path to your customers' door. I know which you're going to choose.

Armed with everything you have learnt about your customers, you're ideally positioned to seize the best content opportunities by focussing your thoughts in the right areas. Go ahead and start planning your tactics.

12

PUBLISHING CHANNELS

"If you're walking down the right path
and you're willing to keep walking,
eventually you'll make progress."

Barack Obama

How can you seize opportunities to dominate publishing channels as they emerge? Equally, how can you make the most of existing channels and continually evolve with your audience's needs?

FINDING YOUR PLACE

Creating and sourcing fantastic content is hard work, so it is vital that you maximise your return by publishing it where it will get the most exposure.

So far, you have talked extensively about creating content that targets specific personas and stages of the buyer's journey, so it makes little sense to spread it thinly across lots of different channels indiscriminately. You need to be smarter than that.

THE 'SITUATIONAL ANALYSIS'

Before you do anything, you need to have a clear understanding of the current shape you're in. What channels do you have already? What is working and what is not? This will help you to prioritise, budget and plan your next moves.

Joe Pulizzi, founder and CEO of the Content Marketing Institute, calls this stage the "situational analysis".

At this point, all of the information you have accumulated so far, including your buyer personas and buyer's journey, will help to reveal the channels where you can have the most impact with your story. What does your research tell you about the platforms your audience prefers to use?

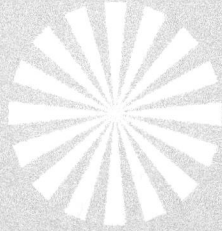

PUBLISHING ACTION

In order to help create an appropriate publishing strategy, ask yourself the following three questions:

1. What do you already have that helps you tell this story (e.g. an existing website, blog, Facebook page, Twitter account, corporate materials, etc.)?
2. What must change in order for you to tell this story (e.g. do you need to add a blog, develop a separate blog, create or revisit your social web strategy)?
3. What must stop (if anything) for you to tell this story (e.g. do you need to stop using Facebook and divert your energy to a blog)?

ALIGNING OBJECTIVES

How do the specific objectives you have attached to each piece of content look against the various channels? Do any particular channels seem to align with, or naturally complement, these objectives?

For example, if one of your goals is to increase brand awareness and the objective for a specific piece of content is to earn 50 social mentions of your brand name, the logical channel might be Twitter.

Some content will fit into more than one channel; if necessary, list primary, secondary and tertiary channels (e.g. primary: YouTube; secondary: brand website; tertiary: Metacafe). Remember, you're only thinking about where the content will physically live, rather than the channels you will use to share or promote it.

DOMINATE, DON'T STAGNATE

You want to dominate conversations and become a big voice in your field, but you can only do this if you have enough impact in the right places. Spreading your efforts thinly across every channel could dilute your rewards.

From a practical point of view, content that is fragmented across many low-use channels is at risk of being forgotten about and stagnating where it sits. This can actually give the impression you have less content available than you do. For example, if you publish one presentation on SlideShare and don't publish again on the channel for 12 months, customers that only touch that channel will think you're inactive.

TO OWN, OR NOT TO OWN

I always feel uneasy when publishing significant volumes of content to third-party-operated platforms. The impending danger is the provider will change publishing rules, limit traffic or visibility of your content, or even introduce (or increase) fees. Wherever there is a toss-up between an owned channel, such as your website or blog, and a rented platform, such as LinkedIn or Facebook, I would personally err towards owned.

PIVOT & STREAMLINE

Whether you're at the start of your content marketing journey, or you are already heavily engaged, it is important that you continually review your use of publishing channels as a matter of course.

The social listening tools you set up earlier as part of your research should be an on-going concern. Where are your customers seeking and accessing content? Think about how your customers' needs are evolving over time and how this ties in with the latest developments in technology and communication trends.

New channels are constantly emerging and often become popular with niche audiences at considerable pace, just as more established channels can wane in popularity overnight.

The market is fluid, so you need to mirror that in your approach to publishing channels. Be ready to kill off failing tactics and seize new opportunities in response to feedback, analytics and evolving behaviours and needs.

MISSION SUMMARY

Think of your publishing channels as the home of your content. This is where it lives 100% of the time it exists, so you need to make sure it can easily be found and accessed by your target audience at key moments of their journey.

At the end of the day, you're aiming to fundamentally influence the way your target customers think about (and interact with) your brand. If you have any hope of attracting enough attention to drive this change, you need to make sure you're talking to enough of the right people, at the right time, in the *right places*.

Always remember, effective communication lines will form the backbone of your revolution. Choose carefully.

13

CONTENT AMPLIFICATION

"Little things make big things happen."

John Wooden

Content amplification is about increasing the reach of your content by employing marketing tactics; it's about marketing your content marketing. It sounds like an odd concept, but bear with me...

TIME FOR YOUR PAY-OFF

You have invested a lot of time so far in researching, planning and producing content, so now you need to maximise your return by getting it out there to as much of your target audience as possible.

Your aim is to magnify its profile so it can rise above everything else out there that is distracting your audience.

Some of your amplification options are relatively low effort and low cost, while others require more work and, in some cases, financial outlay. You'll look more closely at some of your options in just a minute.

AN OBJECTIVE STEER

As we've repeatedly discussed so far, every single piece of content you create has its own specific objectives. You need to consider what you want to achieve with each piece. Are you aiming to drive more traffic back to the website? Do you want to boost brand exposure? Is the aim to grow authority in a specific area?

Before you start to turn up the volume of your voice, it's important that you take the time to estimate just how much exposure the content is likely to need in order to fulfil its purpose. Look at the metrics you attached to your objectives for each piece. With this in mind, you can think about what platforms and amplification methods will be most appropriate.

AMPLIFICATION TYPES

There are three main types of platform for amplification: 'owned media', 'paid media' and 'earned media', with a fusion in the middle, known as 'converged media'.

Figure 12: Converging amplification methods

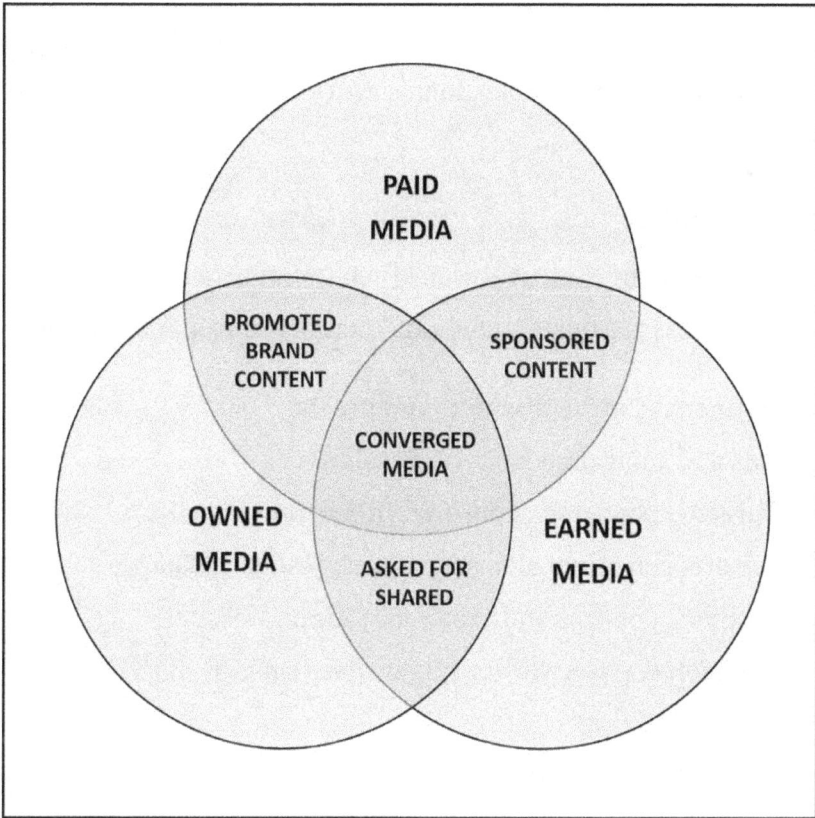

1. OWNED MEDIA

The content that your brand has complete control over is known as owned media. Examples include platforms you own, such as:

- Blog sites, websites and microsites.
- Social profiles, such as Twitter, Facebook, LinkedIn and Google Plus.
- Email distribution lists.

The main benefit of owned media is that you can publish and promote anything you want, in any format, often at very little cost. The downside for most businesses is that it's more difficult to get attention and it usually takes longer to work than paid or earned media.

2. PAID MEDIA

Paying to promote content can help you to quickly generate more exposure across various channels and platforms. Examples include:

- Promoted Twitter accounts and tweets.
- Ads and sponsored posts on Facebook.
- Targeted posts and sponsored InMail on LinkedIn.
- Adverts above and alongside search results on Google.
- Banners, pop-ups and expanding ads on websites.
- Sponsored posts within other sites, such as BuzzFeed and Huffington Post.
- Sponsored and display advertising on YouTube.
- Embedded content or banners within apps.

The main benefits of promoting content on paid channels are much greater reach and faster rates of content propagation. On the flipside, paid media will be seen as advertising (and often dismissed) by your audience if it isn't pitched and targeted perfectly.

3. EARNED MEDIA

This is content that is spread by third parties through activities like PR and word of mouth. Earned media has 'viral' tendencies which often proliferate through social mentions, shares, reposts, reviews and recommendations. Examples include:

- Social sharing.
- Guest blogging.
- References and links from bloggers.
- Mentions and retweets by influencers.
- Press coverage.

The great thing about earned media is that it means others are actively promoting or engaging with your content. Remember that neutral, third-party voices create authentic social proof for your brand. The difficulty with earned media is the fact that you can't buy or create it; rather you have to optimise your content for engagement and sharing.

4. CONVERGED MEDIA

Converged media mixes owned, earned and/or paid platforms. This convergence between media types is the amplification sweet spot. This is where you are able to get the best of all three platform types by setting them to work together seamlessly.

By aiming for a converged media approach to amplification, you can dramatically reduce your financial investment. You can get your amplification strategy off to a start by using owned media to generate earned media.

It is smart to start new content campaigns with owned media and then gauge the effectiveness of the content. You can then decide whether or not to implement paid media tactics to further accelerate amplification.

OPTIMISING FOR EARNED

Whenever you are creating content, you should be thinking about how you can optimise it for earned media. How you can make the content as attractive to your audience as possible, while also maximising its shareability?

This is where you need to put your journalist's hat on.

Use the most attractive and highly-relevant titles, images and propositions that will entice your target customers. But, you must not use gutter press tactics; keep your brand values at the heart of everything you do and remember that no amount of attention is worth eroding your reputation. Always avoid tricking your audience with 'click baiting' tactics, such as misleading headlines or empty promises.

When promoting the content, you also need to sow some seeds to encourage advocates and influencers to interact with your content and share it with their own audience. You can start by making sure they are aware of the content. For example, could you target a specific piece of content towards a key influencer on Twitter, using mentions and relevant hashtags?

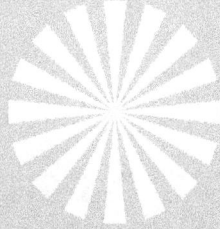

AMPLIFICATION ACTION

Think about the buyer's journey you mapped out earlier. What do your buyer personas and market research tell you about where your audience is at each stage of the journey? Make a list of the media channels they are using to find solutions to their problems.

Your amplification tactics should support all of these stages, from Awareness and Discovery through to the Consideration, Purchase and Advocate and Reconvert stages.

COUP INSIGHT

There are a number of tools that can help you to manage your content amplification activities and also make it easier for your customers to share your content. Tools to consider include:

- **AddThis** allows you to implement simple ways for visitors to share content from your owned channels, such as share buttons that allow content to be distributed across multiple platforms and social networks, driving traffic back to your website.

- **Outbrain** is a content discovery platform that helps to promote articles, videos, slideshows, infographics, and even earned media across high-traffic, well-known media properties, such as CNN, Slate and ESPN.

- **Zemanta** compiles original content and then optimises it for multiple distribution hubs, such as promoted recommendations, in-stream advertisements, in-text ads, and sponsored content on top media sites.

- **Cision** provides tools to create, publish, drive, and analyse branded content. By targeting engaged audiences on top-tier websites, it aims to increase brand exposure and drive traffic.

MISSION SUMMARY

Ultimately, content amplification is about connecting dots. It's about linking your content to your target audience, in the right places, at optimal moments.

Of course, the more you understand your audience and their journey, the better informed your amplification tactics will be. Let all of the insights you have gathered so far give you the confidence to experiment with techniques and adapt your approach as you go. Remember, content rarely achieves massive reach just by chance; it's usually the result of a heightened understanding of the audience and a series of educated risks.

Be bold, have courage and never rely on blind hope!

14

MEASURING & MONITORING

"A good decision is based on knowledge
and not on numbers."

Plato

When you're setting goals, it is important to remember that every single one of them needs to be measurable. Furthermore, your metrics have to specifically tell you something about the value of every single one of your activities.

Most businesses fall down by looking too broadly at general numbers like page views and shares, without interpreting this data into actionable insights. Use this as an opportunity to get ahead of your competitors by only collecting valuable, actionable insights.

The only way to accurately measure your success is to constantly relate the metrics you gather to the overall aims, goals and objectives of your content marketing activities. Rather than just reporting raw figures like website visits, video views, and social interactions, you need to create a narrative interpretation of your performance.

CAPTURING LEADS

So far, you have talked about improving your brand image, getting on your audience's radar and building confidence in your product. But what is it all for ultimately? You want to convert your content users into customers, so you have to look specifically at how much impact you're having on lead generation.

Of course, it's difficult to directly attribute your content marketing activity to sales figures, as, by definition, it doesn't usually direct customers to the buy button. However, you can (and should) be tracking the leads that your activity is generating.

You will now take a closer look at the impact your content marketing activity is having on lead generation:

- **Email subscriptions:** Along with measuring the number of subscriptions to newsletters, you can feed names and other details you capture directly into your email marketing system, for example MailChimp or Pure 360. This information goes some of the way towards indicating how your subscribers relate to the buyer personas you were targeting. Did you attract the types of customers you set out to?

- **Downloads:** Quite easily, you can track the number of 'open downloads' (where a customer doesn't have to enter any details to access the content) by setting up 'Events' in Google Analytics. For 'gated downloads' (where the customer has to enter some details before they can access the content), you can, again, feed the information you capture into your email marketing system or your CRM (client relationship management system), such as Salesforce or Zoho. This enables you to track the progress of your relationship with the lead following this interaction with your content.

- **Enquiries and call backs:** By adding Google Analytics 'Events' code to specific links, you can pin down the specific piece of content a prospect was referred by. To track telephone enquiries, you can either set up specific telephone numbers to channel enquiries that originate from content, or build in questions to the telephone operators' script.

- **Referrals:** By using features that allow your audience to refer (or send) content to friends or colleagues, you can capture lead data from both the sender and receiver, also feeding this directly into your CRM.

MARKET AUTOMATION

While analytics platforms like Google Analytics and Web Trends can provide numbers and highlight behavioural patterns, this information is not tied to specific individuals. You can dig a lot deeper using market automation systems like Marketo, Hubspot and Eloqua. These systems harvest reliable lead data by tracking specific individuals as they travel through the buyer's journey, even scoring how 'hot' each lead is by interpreting their behavioural characteristics.

Market automation systems don't come cheap, with annual subscriptions typically between $10,000 and $50,000, but if budget allows, they offer highly detailed reporting capabilities.

BRAND PERCEPTIONS

The best way to measure how perceptions of your brand are changing is by looking at the sentiments of interactions across social media. Are you increasing favourable mentions and reducing negative ones?

You can conduct a study into awareness of your brand and products as a result of your content marketing activity. There are a number of standalone tools that can help you with sentiment analysis (also known as opinion mining), including some built into social platforms (such as Facebook). These tools analyse qualitative metrics, based around the use of words in relation to attitudes, emotions and opinions. Look at Radian6, Social Mention and free custom dashboards in Netvibes.

TRAFFIC

While traffic doesn't always equate to sales, it does tell you whether your content activities are generating interest in your products and services. You can use Google Analytics to look at the volume of traffic visiting your websites, along with measuring product-related touch-points, such as app usage and any customer enquiry data you can gather.

By looking specifically at where traffic is coming from, you can work out exactly what content is having the most leverage across the buyer's journey.

Are there any signs that you are creating a buzz around your brand? Is your content strengthening the link between your company and your product area? To help you answer these questions, you can look for increases in searches for the types of products you offer that include your brand name.

TIME IS OF THE ESSENCE

One way to measure how engaged your audience is with specific pieces of content is by looking at how much time they spend on it. Look at things like time-on-page data from Google Analytics and video view durations in YouTube. Surprisingly, less than half of all marketers measure this kind of data, according to research by Contently.

SOCIAL TRACTION

By measuring the social interactions each piece of content generates, you can better understand how deeply it is resonating with the target audience. How many tweets, retweets, likes, shares, comments and mentions is each piece earning? What are the channels and amplification platforms that are showing the most activity?

Here, you're interested in spikes in activity across all social platforms. What are you doing specifically that is generating this interest and what are you getting out of it? For example, are these spikes either leading web traffic to other content in your portfolio or generating email subscribers, customer enquiries or even purchases? Understanding this will help you to focus your efforts on the activities that generate those 'hot actions' among your target audience.

DOWN TO BRASS TACKS

How much is all of this engagement worth versus the time and money you have invested? You can use all of the lead data you have gathered to report the sales-lift among customers that have been exposed to your content marketing activity.

Whether you're spending money on content generation or using company hours, you need to report just how much you're spending versus the amount of engagement you're generating in return.

REPORTING

Although you'll measure and monitor each piece of content continuously, you'll need to report more broadly on your activities at certain points.

The main purpose of reporting is to demonstrate the impact you're having on the business as a whole. You'll do this by pulling together all of the data you have gathered and creating a narrative that interprets the results. Remember to frame all of your metrics within the context of specific aims, goals and objectives.

MEASURING & MONITORING ACTION

Gather all of the analytics you have available for one single piece of content.

Using both qualitative and quantitative data, write a short report explaining how things like the number of social interactions indicate that the content has been successful. Use your data to show how these numbers prove that the content is or isn't driving the actions you were aiming for. Explain what spikes in customer activity may tell you about the resonance of a certain topic.

By writing a narrative around your measurement data, you will be in a better position to work out the things you're doing well and the things you need to change. Of course, it will also help you to judge whether you're measuring the right things.

MISSION SUMMARY

At the end of the day, you need to be able to answer one question: did it work?

I can't stress enough how important it is to focus only on metrics that directly relate to your big aim, goals and objectives. Don't waste time collecting data and reporting on anything else. In my experience, information that doesn't prove or justify your activity will just distract you from those actionable nuggets of insight, not to mention bloat your reports and encourage extraneous questions from above that are impossible to answer.

In a nutshell, by focussing on the right things, you'll keep your wits sharp and feel more empowered to cut loose ineffective efforts that are slowing you down.

The concept is simple: collect the right information, make informed judgements and change things that aren't working. Your mantra goes like this: 'GAUGE - ACT – MEASURE – ADAPT'.

GLOSSARY

AFFINITY DIAGRAMS

An 'affinity diagram' (also known as 'affinity' chart or the 'KJ Method') is a tool used to organise ideas and data by sorting them into groups.

ATTITUDINAL VARIABLES

'Attitudinal variables' are representations of the feelings a specific group of people have on a particular topic. These attitudes (such as likes and dislikes) are usually derived from surveys and interviews with a sample set of people, which can then be mapped across a spectrum.

BIG AIM

The overarching purpose of the strategy as a whole is known as the 'big aim'. This is the primary focus of what the mission sets out to accomplish. The big aim should be supported by a series of supporting goals, which are then subsequently split into objectives and tactics.

BUSINESS CASE

The 'business case' is a formal argument (usually both written and presented in-person) for pursuing a specific course of action, using examples and supporting information. The business case is targeted towards the key decision maker(s) in an organisation.

BUYER PERSONAS

'Buyer personas' (also known as 'customer personas') are fictional characters that are created to represent real customer or audience groups. Personas aim to represent customer types, grouped according to their needs and motivations. They are used for a variety of purposes in marketing, such as customer targeting and user experience planning for digital projects.

BUYER'S JOURNEY

The 'buyer's journey' is made up of the stages that every customer goes through before buying a product, from becoming aware of their need to making a purchase. Although not all customers will spend the same amount of time at each stage, the process will largely be the same.

CONTENT AMPLIFICATION

Promoting, highlighting and marketing content in order to reach the largest possible audience across one or more publishing channels is known as 'Content amplification'.

CONTENT AUDIT

A 'content audit' is the evaluation of all content within a specific portfolio, usually including individual quality assessment and specific recommendations. A content audit is usually conducted in conjunction with a 'content inventory' (see below).

CONTENT CALENDAR

A 'content calendar' is a plan that specifies production and publication dates of content over a period of time. Content calendars vary in complexity and formats (paper-based or web/software-based), usually according to the volume and scale of the schedule.

CONTENT COMMUNITY

The 'content community' is a collection of individuals, groups or brands that have an interest in a specific topic. A content community typically includes customers, product or brand champions and competitors.

CONTENT CURATION

Gathering, filtering and selectively republishing content that has been produced by a third-party is known as 'content curation'. The content must not be republished in its entirety and the terms of publishing should be beneficial to both the original publisher and the curator.

CONTENT FORMAT

The 'content format' is the technical make-up of the content, e.g. PDF, print, webpage, MP3. Not to be confused with 'content type' (see below).

CONTENT INVENTORY

A 'content inventory' is a complete catalogue of the entire contents of a website, including a record of whether the content is currently published and its location. A content inventory is usually conducted in conjunction with a 'content audit' (see above).

CONTENT MARKETING

The term 'content marketing' refers to marketing activities that involve the creation and distribution of useful or stimulating content in order to acquire and retain customers, without overtly selling a product or brand.

CONTENT NICHE

A 'content niche' is the highly-specific topic specialism that a publisher focuses attention on. Publishers tend to focus on niche topics in order to influence customer attitudes and needs, while gaining authority in an area that aligns with their specific knowledge or expertise.

CONTENT TYPE

The 'content type' is the kind of content that is being published, e.g. blog post, web page, video, whitepaper or leaflet. The content type is not to be confused with the 'content format' (see above).

CONVERGED MEDIA

'Converged media' is content that is amplified (or distributed) through a combination of at least two amplification methods, e.g. paid media, owned media and/or earned media.

EARNED MEDIA

The term 'earned media' (also known as 'free media') refers to content that is amplified (or distributed) through publicity, editorial influence and other promotional tactics that are not paid for. Examples include: news articles, features and social shares, mentions and reposts.

INFLUENCERS

'Influencers' are individuals, groups and brands that have dominant voices in their field. Their ideas and views have the power to shape other people's opinions and drive actions.

OWNED MEDIA

'Owned media' is content that is amplified (or distributed) across channels that are within your control, such as websites, blogs, or email. Typically, owned media is free to publish. Examples include: content published to proprietary websites, apps and blogs.

PAID MEDIA

Content that is amplified (or distributed) with paid-for advertising or promotion is known as 'paid media'. Examples include: pay-per-click, display advertising, sponsored posts, paid influencers, social media advertisements and retargeting.

PUBLISHING CHANNELS

The places content is published, such as websites, blog sites, email and social platforms such as Facebook, Twitter, and YouTube, are known as 'publishing channels'.

REAL-TIME PUBLISHING

The term 'real-time publishing' refers to agile content production and publishing that typically aim to influence customer conversations as they happen. Real-time publishing is influenced by current trends and developing topics within specific topic areas.

SEARCH ENGINE OPTIMISATION

The term 'search engine optimisation' refers to the process of maximising the number of visitors to a particular website or piece of content. This typically includes effectively using relevant keywords in a structure and format that search engines, such as Google, will recognise as relevant targeted search queries.

SOCIAL MEDIA

Websites and applications that enable users to create and share content or to participate in social networking are known as 'social media'.

STYLE GUIDE

A 'style guide' (also sometimes known as 'brand standards') is a set of guidelines to help publishers create content that is consistent in look, quality, tone and appearance. These guidelines typically include basic information about editorial uniformity, brand personality and visual identity.

REFERENCE LINKS

1. AddThis, http://www.addthis.com

2. Any Meeting, http://www.anymeeting.com

3. Ask MetaFilter, http://ask.metafilter.com

4. Blaze, http://www.blazecontent.com

5. Book Baby, http://www.bookbaby.com

6. BrandWatch, http://www.brandwatch.com

7. Buyer Persona Manifesto, http://www.buyerpersona.com

8. Cam Studio, http://www.camstudio.org

9. Cision, http://www.cision.com

10. Click Webinar, http://www.clickwebinar.com

11. Clickz, http://www.clickz.com

12. Content Marketing Institute,

    http://www.contentmarketinginstitute.com

13. Content Marketing Coup,

    http://www.contentmarketingcoup.com

14. Contently, http://www.contently.com

15. Create Space, http://www.createspace.com

16. Curata, http://www.curata.com

17. Delicious, http://www.delicious.com

18. DemandGen, http://www.demandgen.com

19. DemandMetric, http://www.demandmetric.com

20. Digg, http://www.digg.com

21. Eloqua, http://www.eloqua.com

22. Facebook, http://www.facebook.com

23. Feedley, http://www.feedly.com

24. Gather Content, http://www.gathercontent.com

25. Go Animate, http://www.goanimate.com

26. Google Alerts, http://www.google.co.uk/alerts

27. Google Analytics, http://www.google.co.uk/analytics

28. Google Docs, http://www.google.co.uk/docs/about/

29. Google Keyword Planner,

http://adwords.google.com/keywordplanner

30. Google Plus, http://plus.google.com

31. Google Trends, http://www.google.co.uk/trends

32. Hootsuite, http://www.hootsuite.com

33. Hubspot, http://www.hubsot.com

34. Imgflip, http:// www.imgflip.com

35. IMN, http://www.imninc.com

36. Infogram, http://www.infogr.am

37. Instagram, http//www.instagram.com

38. Klout, http://www.klout.com

39. LinkedIn, http://www.linkedin.com

40. MailChimp, http://www.mailchimp.com

41. Meerkat, http://www.meerkatapp.co

42. Meme Generator, http://www.memegenerator.net

43. Mention, http://www.en.mention.com

44. Netvibes, http://www.netvibes.com

45. Outbrain, http://www.outbrain.com

46. Paper.li, http://www.paper.li

47. Piktochart, http://www.piktochart.com

48. Pinterest, http:http://www.pinterest.com

49. Pixton, http://www.pixton.com

50. Pure 360, http://www.pure360.com

51. QuickSprout, http://www.quicksprout.com

52. Quora, http://www.quora.com

53. Radian6, http://www.radian6.com

54. Salesforce, http://www.salesforce.com

55. ScoopIt, http://www.scoop.it

56. Screaming Frog, http://www.screamingfrog.co.uk

57. Screencast-O-Matic, http://www.screencast-o-matic.com

58. SEMrush, http://www.semrush.com

59. Shared Count, http://www.sharedcount.com

60. SlideShare, http://www.slideshare.net

61. Social Mention, http://www.socialmention.com

62. Socialcrawlytics, http://www.socialcrawlytics.com

63. Static Brain, http://www.statisticbrain.com

64. Swayy, http://www.swayy.co

65. Talkwalker Alerts, http://www.talkwalker.com/alerts

66. The Tweeted Times, http://www.tweetedtimes.com

67. Traackr, http://www.traackr.com

68. TrapIt, http://www.trap.it

69. Twitter, http://www.twitter.com

70. Unsplash, http://www.unsplash.com

71. Vimeo, http://www.vimeo.com

72. Web Trends, http://www.webtrends.com

73. Wordtracker, http://www.wordtracker.com

74. YouTube, http://www.youtube.com

75. Zemanta, http://www.zemanta.com

76. Zoho, http://www.zoho.com

CONNECT WITH DANE

Website : www.danebrookes.com

Twitter: @danebrookes

ABOUT THE AUTHOR

Dane Brookes is a content marketing and communications specialist, with a broad range of experience that has touched many different sectors and industries.

With a background in business journalism and content strategy, he has produced high-profile marketing and communications campaigns for some of the most influential global brands of the last decade.

At the forefront of the open-access boom, Dane led an editorial department at one of the world's largest publishing houses, before going on to manage digital marketing and communications for a number of high-profile organisations, including a national housing charity, a Russell Group university and a FTSE 100 utility company.

In 2012, he founded marketing and technology company, Group Dane (www.groupdane.com), which has a portfolio of clients in the UK, USA and Europe.

www.ingramcontent.com/pod-product-compliance
Lightning Source LLC
Chambersburg PA
CBHW022039190326
41520CB00008B/640